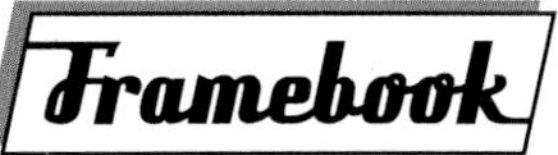

BARRA
& VATERSAY

Dedicated to Eileen & Donald (Scutach) Campbell

ICP

www.iaincampbellphotography.com

About the Author

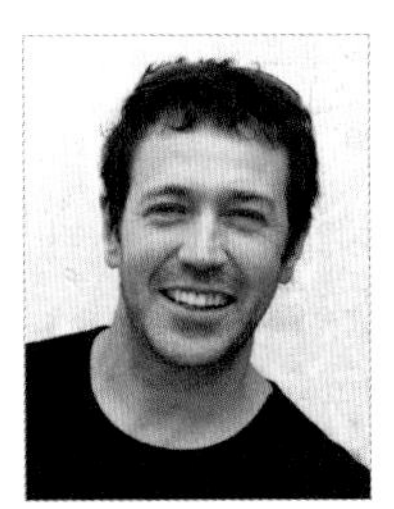

Born in Glasgow in 1967, Iain Kirk Campbell has travelled extensively and lived in Mainland Europe, the Middle East and New Zealand. He has worked in publishing for over 25 years as a photographer, designer and author. A keen walker and mountain biker, he has always felt a strong connection to the landscape, and in particular to the Highlands and Islands of Scotland. The first two books in the ICP Framebook series profiles the Hebridean islands of Skye, and Barra & Vatersay – where Iain's father's family came from.

Barra & Vatersay

ICP Framebook
First published 2015
Second edition published 2019

www.iaincampbellphotography.com

ISBN: 978-0-473-27664-5

Special thanks to Ross and Carol Campbell, Frith Williams and Megan Linwood

Introduction

Sometimes called the Hebrides in miniature, Barra & Vatersay are the smallest and most southerly inhabited islands of Scotland's Outer Hebrides. Perched on the western edge of Europe, these beautiful and remote islands offer a remarkably diverse landscape that belies their tiny size.

To the west and exposed to the full power of the Atlantic Ocean, craggy headlands are interspersed with stunning white-sand beaches. These give way to machair, rare lime-rich grasslands known for their fertility and abundance of summer flowers. The rugged interior is formed mostly of gnarled, granite-studded hills and globally significant areas of blanket peat bog. To the east, rocky inlets and bays predominate, and towering over all is Heaval, which at 383 metres is the islands' tallest peak.

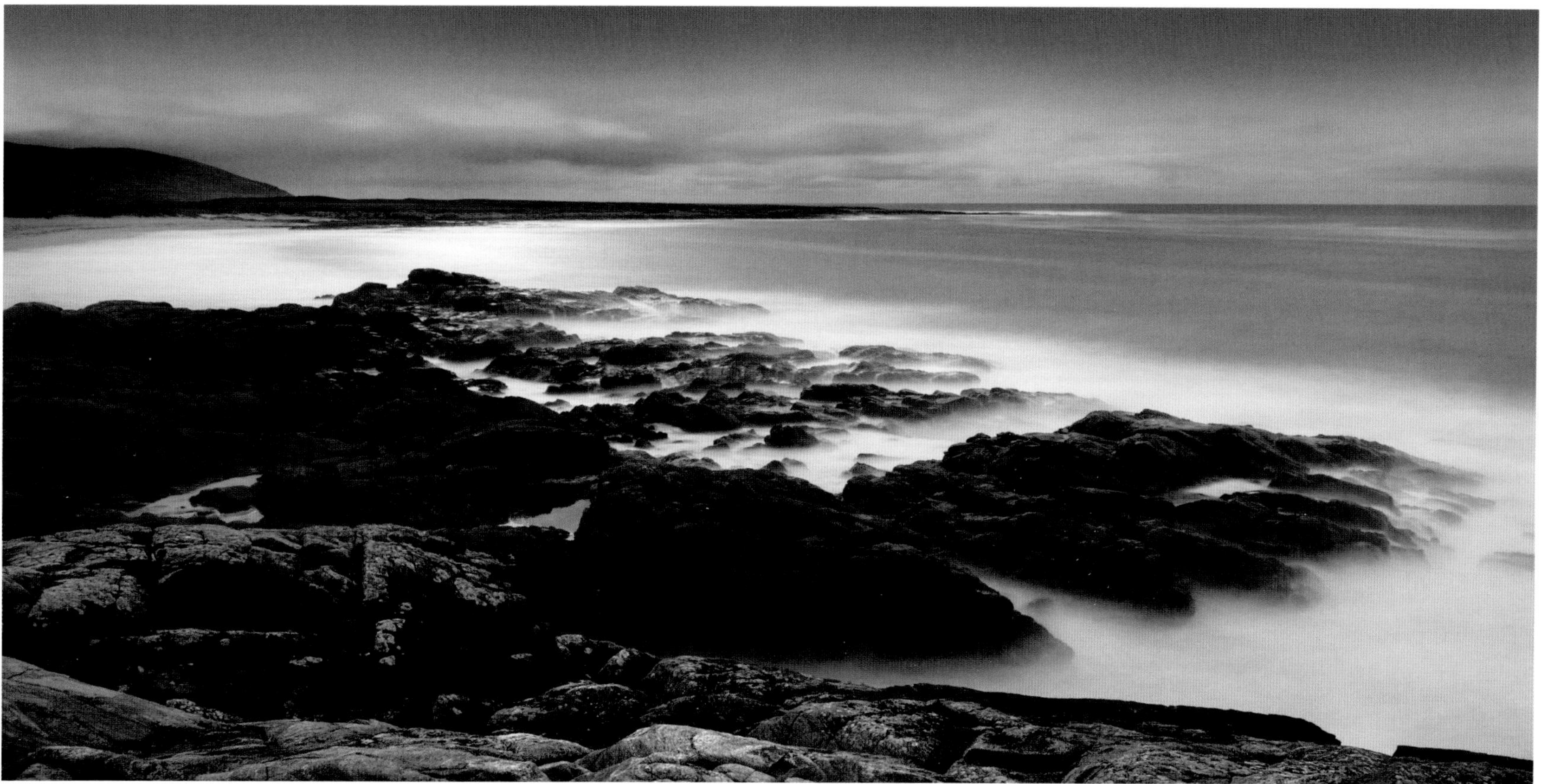

Calm seas at twilight on Barra's west coast

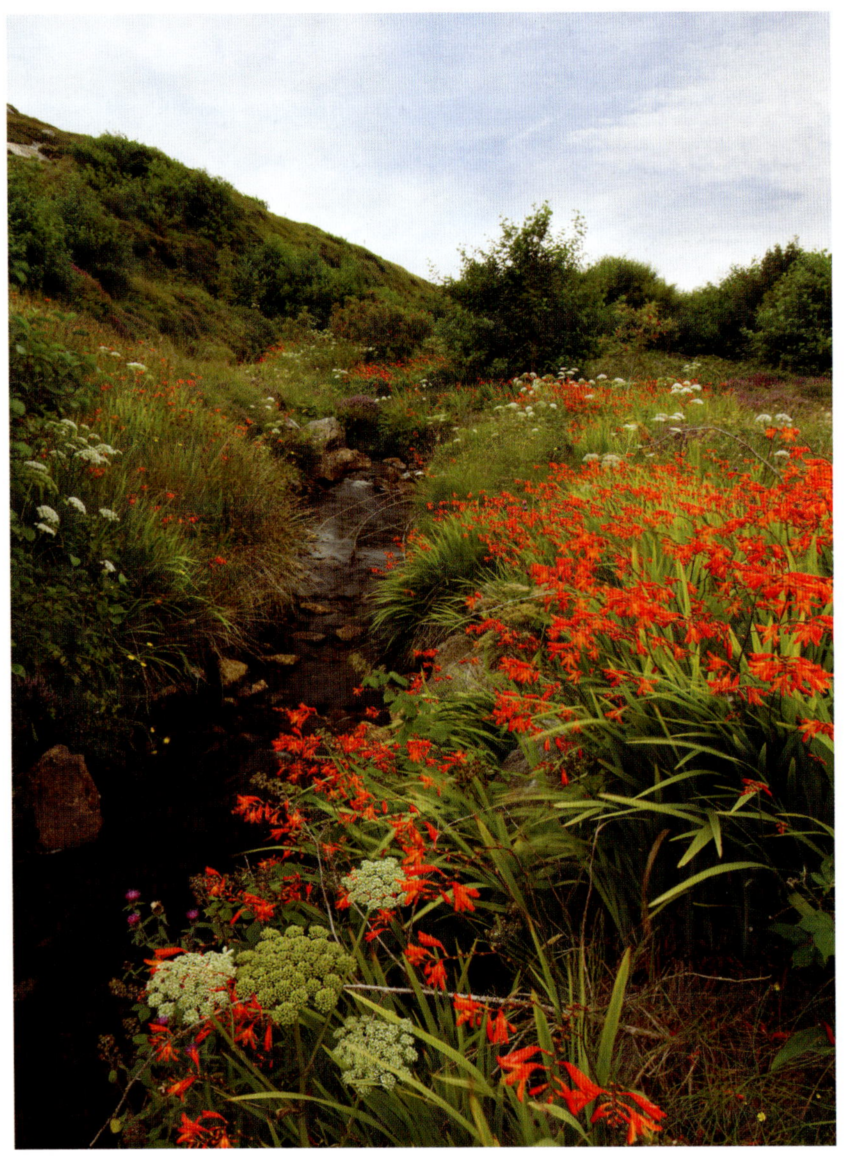

The islands have a rich and colourful history, with evidence of human settlement reaching back at least 6,000 years. Archaeological sites pepper the landscape, from Neolithic standing stones and Iron Age forts to long-abandoned villages. Ancient hunter-gatherers, Celts, Picts, Gaels, Vikings, and even some adventurous English folk have all settled here. Piracy, rebellion, brutal evictions, periods of feast and times of famine have all left their mark on the landscape and on the character of the people.

Today, Barra and Vatersay are archetypal outposts of the kind that fire the imagination. Those seeking respite from the demands of their urban lives, and a pace of life more in tune with the rhythms of nature, will not be disappointed. However, these islands are in no way sleepy backwaters; neither are they ersatz Gaelic theme parks for tourists. They remain real working communities with a strong sense of their own identity. Here on the western fringes of the continent there endures an alternative but equal vitality to that of the big cities, where life is dominated by the raw forces of nature.

About this Framebook

This ICP Framebook seeks to capture the essence of the Barra and Vatersay landscape. Framebooks are designed to allow you to extract the full-page photographs for framing. To this end, there is no text on these pages. If you would prefer to keep the book intact, you can order prints from **www.iaincampbellphotography.com**.

Wild flowers are abundant during the spring and summer months

Right: Tràigh Mhòr, Barra

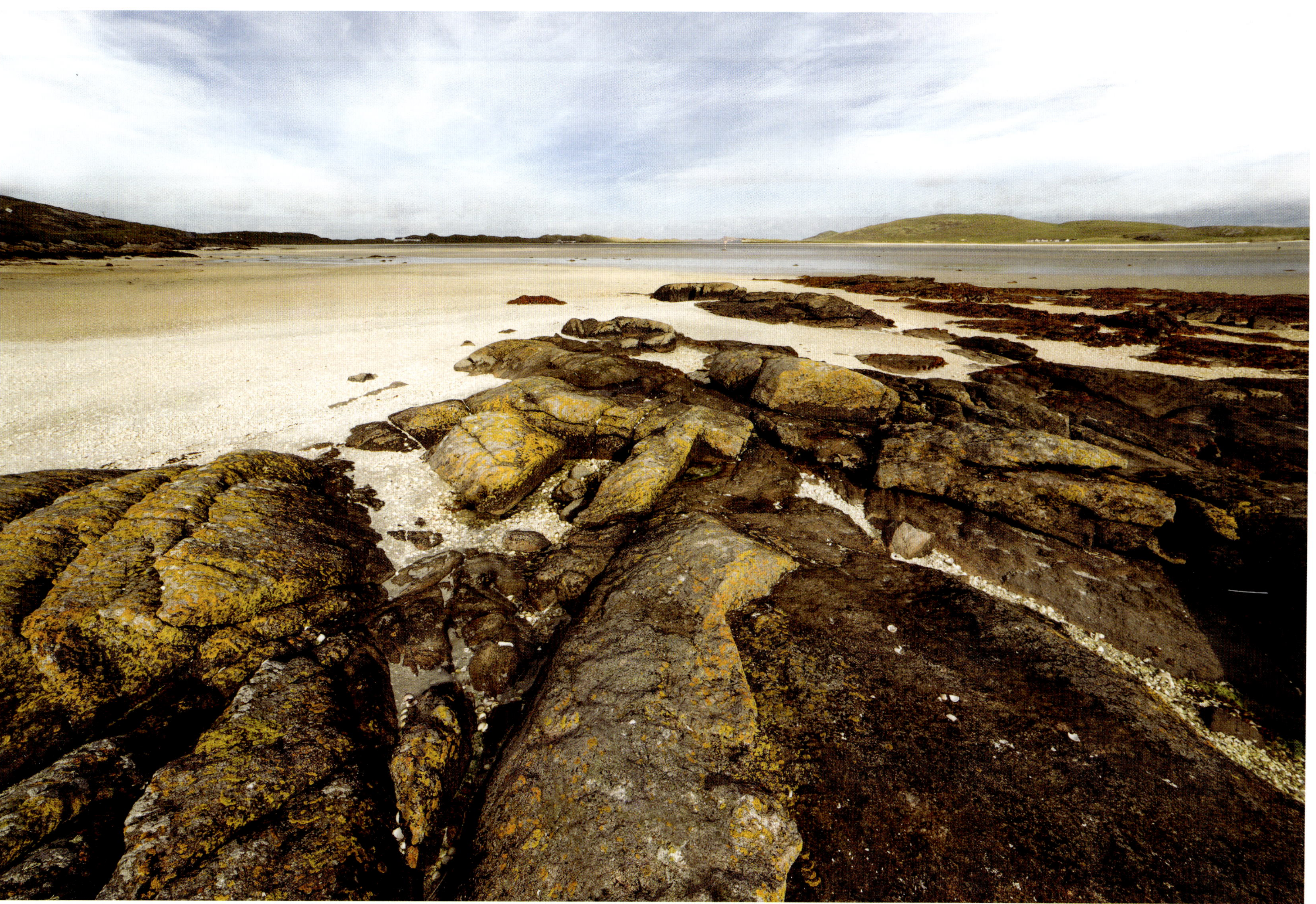

Barra Airport

At the northern end of Barra is the wide, shallow bay of Tràigh Mhòr, home to the world's only airport where scheduled flight times are determined by the tides. The three beach runways, each marked by wooden poles, are twice daily submerged by the high tide. On occasion, emergency night flights have to rely on reflective strips laid on the beach and illuminated by vehicle headlights to define the runway.

Flying into Barra is a unique experience and a spectacular alternative to arriving by sea. Despite often being cited as one of the world's most hair-raising landings, Barra Airport actually has a reassuring safety record and complies with the same regulations as other UK airports. Scheduled flights began in 1936, and today around 10,000 people use the airport annually. Canadian built DHC-6 Twin Otters, designed for short take offs and landings, fly from Glasgow up to twice a day.

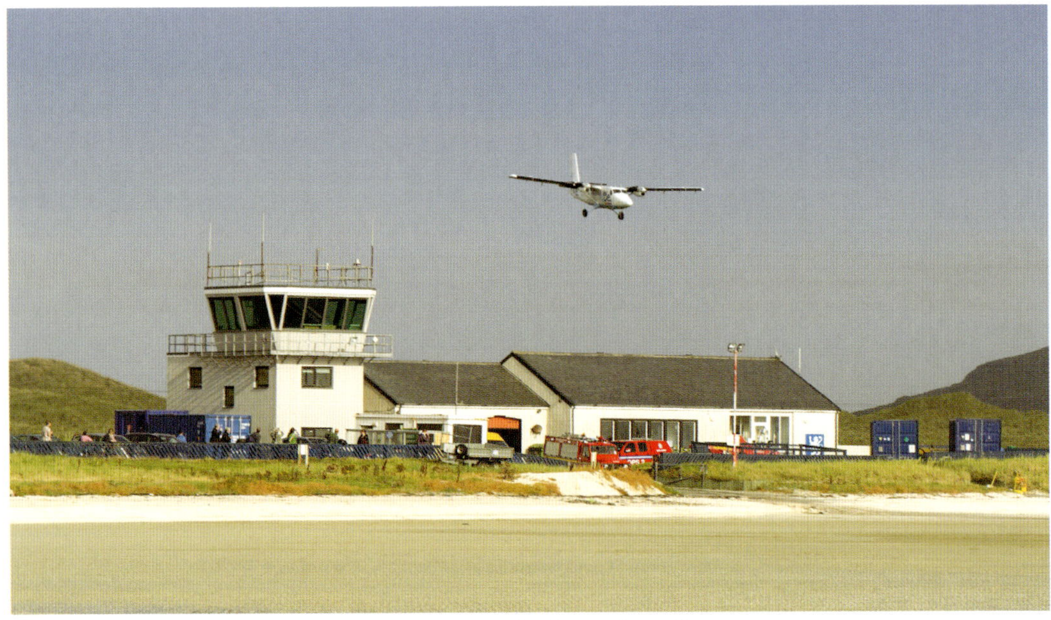

A plane approaches the beach runway over the terminal building at Barra Airport

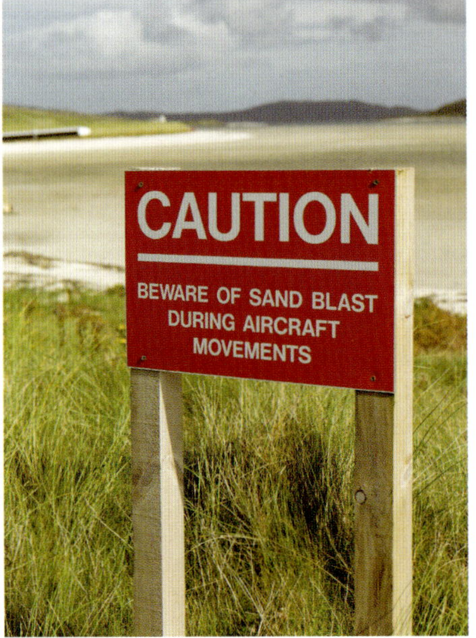

Right: A Twin Otter lands on the sands at Barra Airport

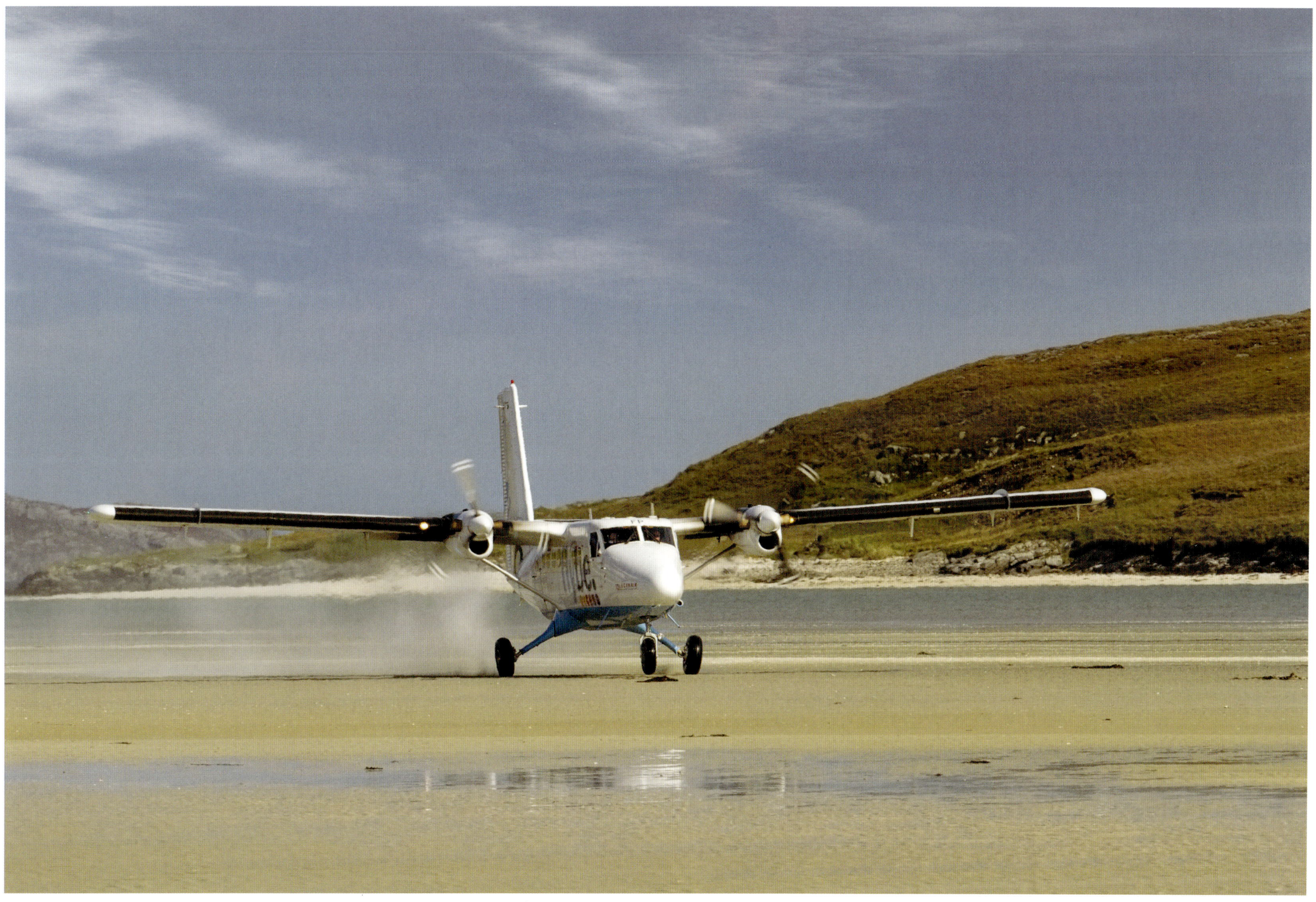

Kisimul Castle

Sitting on a tiny isle in Castlebay Harbour is the iconic Kisimul Castle, historic seat of the MacNeil clan of Barra. With its own fresh water supply via an underground stream, the islet was the perfect site for this strategically important fort in Castlebay – the first safe harbour north of Ireland, and the gateway to the Hebrides.

Kisimul was almost certainly built over the remains of an ancient broch (prehistoric fort), probably in the early 15th century. In the mid-18th century, it was abandoned and fell into ruin. However, substantial renovations were carried out in the 20th century, and today Kisimul is the only significant medieval castle in all the Western Isles.

Visitors are often surprised at how much the MacNeils managed to fit within the castle's defensive curtain walls. Around a small courtyard they built a three-storey tower house, a feasting hall, a chapel, the heir's house, and the watchman's house. Just outside the curtain wall are the ruins of an old galley crew house.

Legend tells of the wily MacNeils tricking Norse besiegers by hanging cowhides smeared with fresh dogs' blood over the castle walls. Originally destined to become shoes, the hides suggested that the MacNeils had a plentiful food supply and convinced the Norsemen to sail away. In all its long history, the castle has never been taken by an enemy.

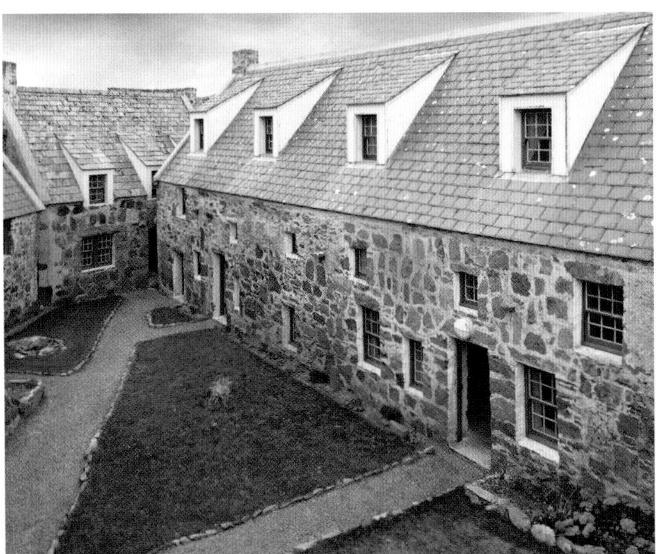
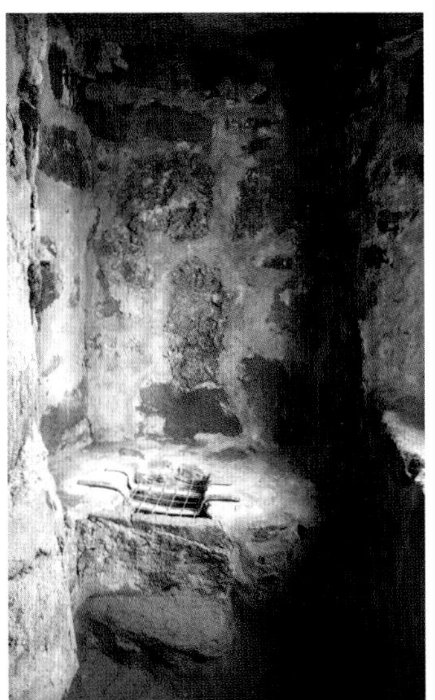

Left: Kisimul Castle's tidy little courtyard. Right: The smallest room in the tower house, flushed twice daily by the tide

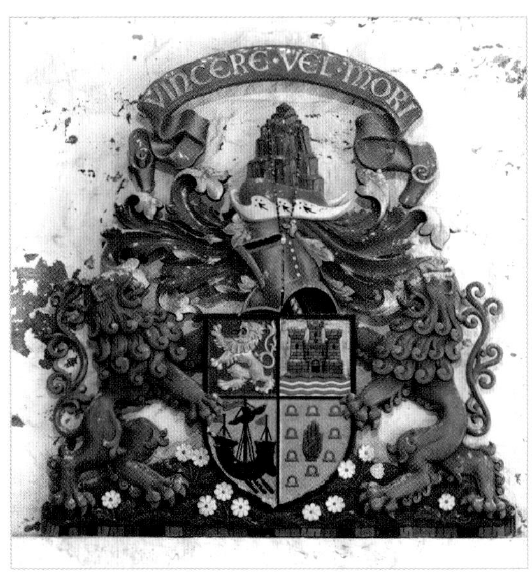

The MacNeils' coat of arms, showing their motto Vincere Vel Mori – Victory or Death

Right: Kisimul Castle, Barra

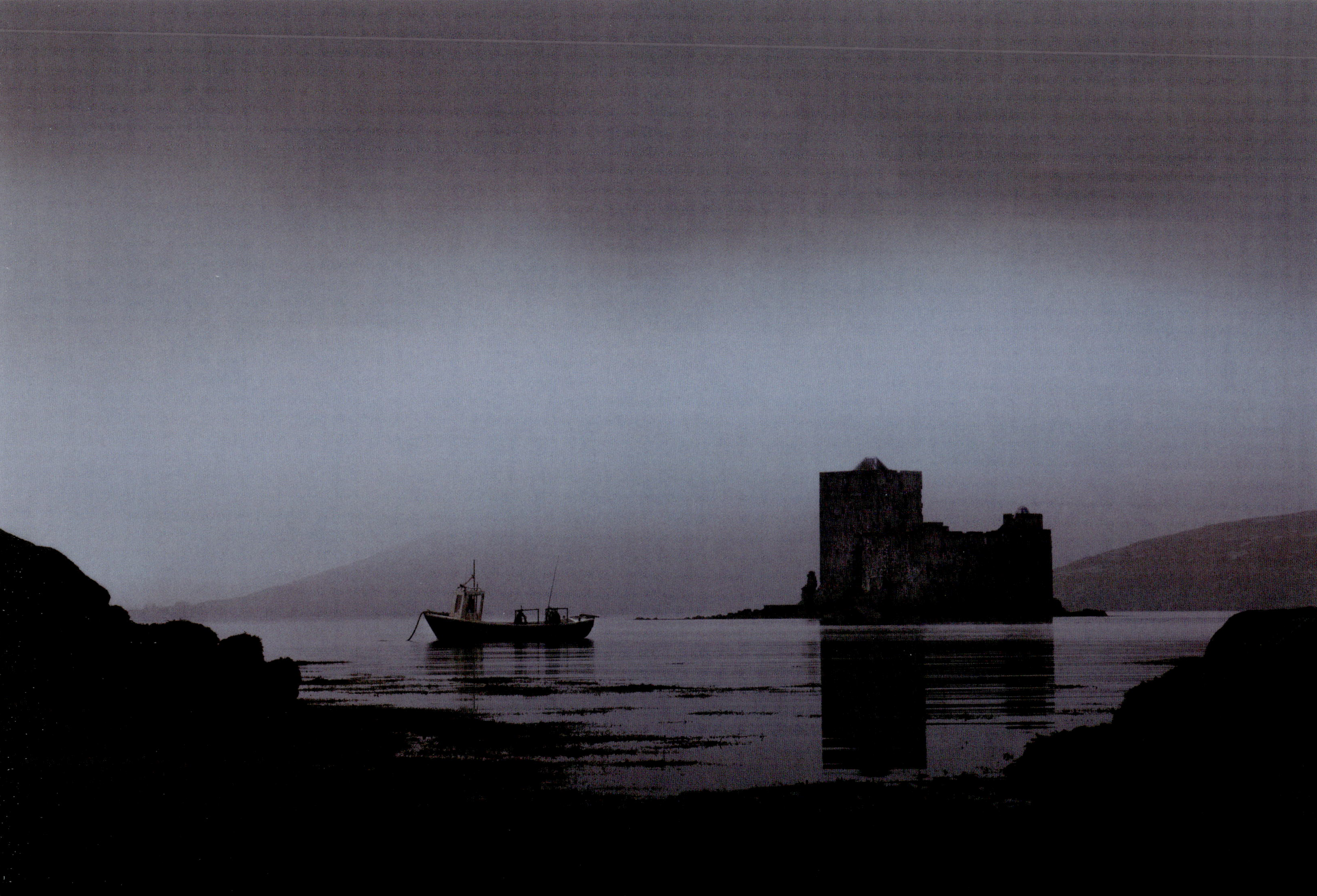

Machair

Seeing the machair in bloom is one of the highlights of a visit to the Outer Hebrides in late spring and summer. Machair is Gaelic for 'fertile plain' and refers to the unique grasslands that fringe many of the Atlantic beaches. One of the rarest environments in Europe, the machair supports a wealth of uncommon wild flowers and is an important habitat to many birds and insects.

Shell sand blown inland from the dunes creates an alkaline soil, which – combined with just the right amount of wind, rain, and seasonal grazing – forms the machair. From mid-May until the end of summer, the pastures are host to stunning carpet blooms. Predominantly white during spring, these give way to yellows in high summer, and red and purple hues as the season draws to a close.

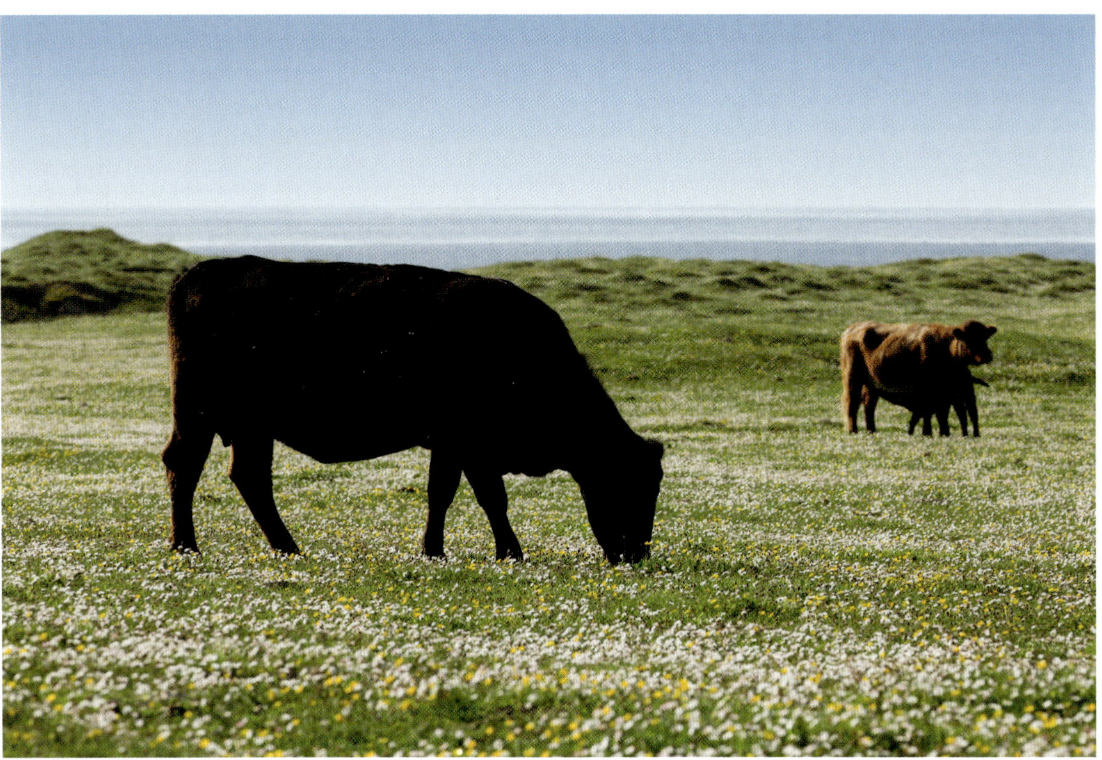

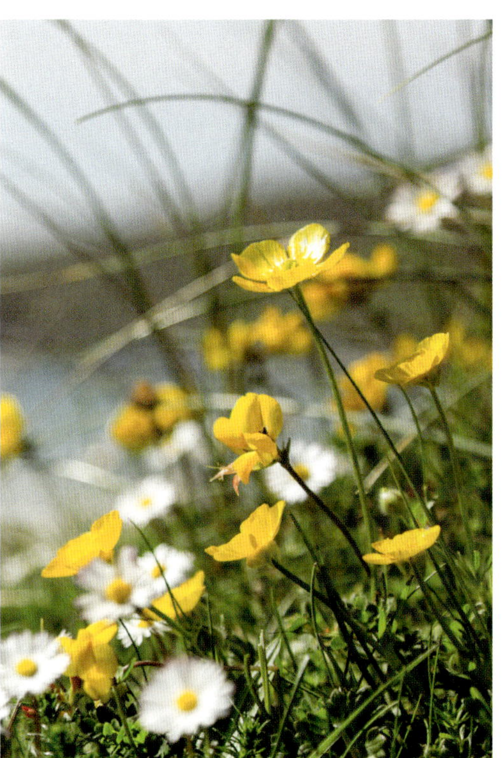

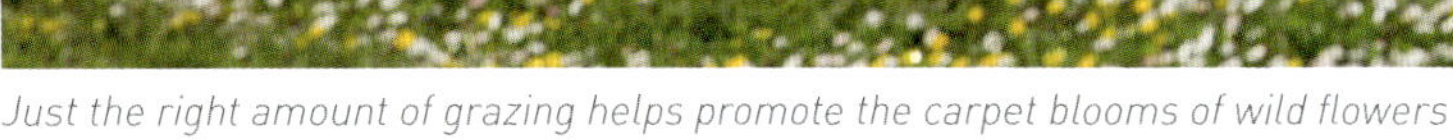
Just the right amount of grazing helps promote the carpet blooms of wild flowers

Right: Machair surrounds the remains of Neolithic standing stones at Borve, Barra

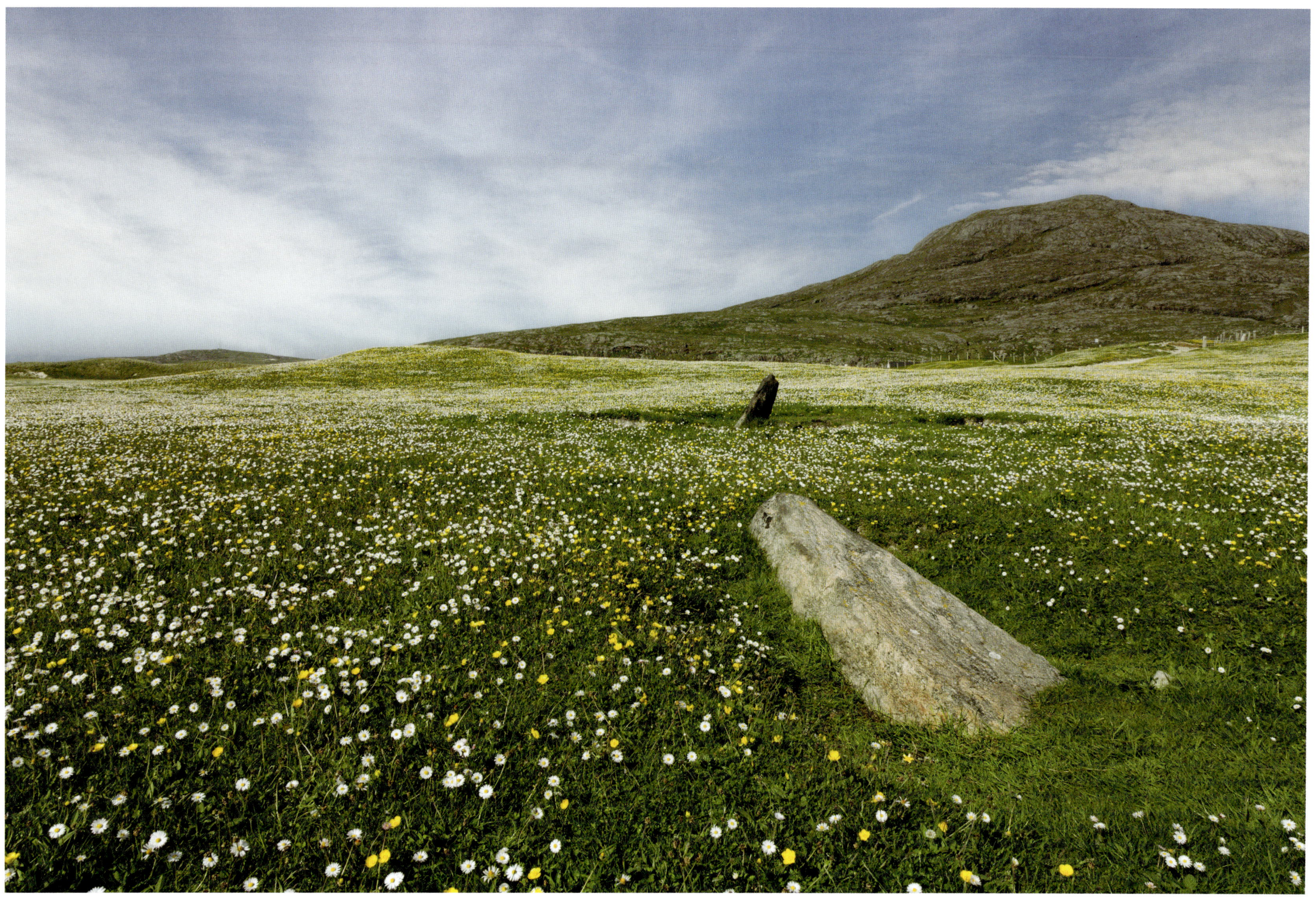

Sea of Faith

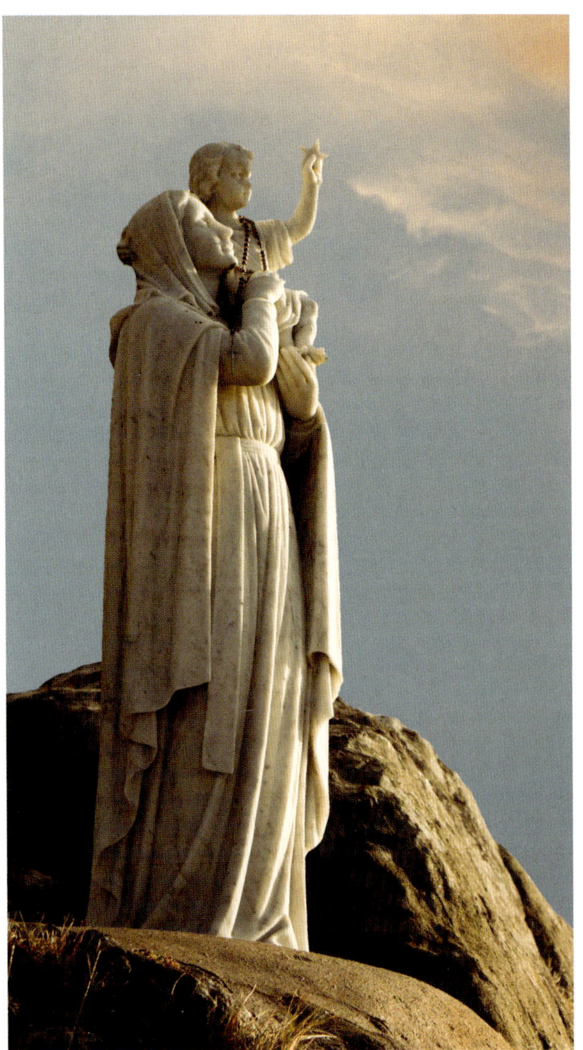

Our Lady of the Sea, Heaval, Barra

Close to the summit of Heaval a white marble statue of the Madonna and Child looks out over Castlebay and the Bishop Isles to the south. Known locally as *Our Lady of the Sea*, it was erected in 1954 and is testament to the islands' predominantly Catholic, seafaring population.

Throughout history, the Hebridean's precarious relationship with the sea has exacted a heavy toll. Unpredictable weather and treacherous rocky shores have spelt the end for many vessels and their crew. The worst maritime disaster to befall the islands was the 1853 sinking of the *Annie Jane*, an immigrant ship on its way from Liverpool to Canada. Caught in a severe storm, it ran aground and broke up near the southern tip of Vatersay's West Bay. Locals managed to save 101 people, but 333 souls were lost. In the 20th century, many of the islands' menfolk were lost during the two world wars while serving in the merchant navy. Far from being a relatively safe posting, the merchant navy suffered horrendous losses and a fatality rate nearly four times that of the other services.

Given the islands' tragic maritime history, *Our Lady of the Sea* brings to mind the adage 'There's no such thing as an atheist on a sinking ship.'

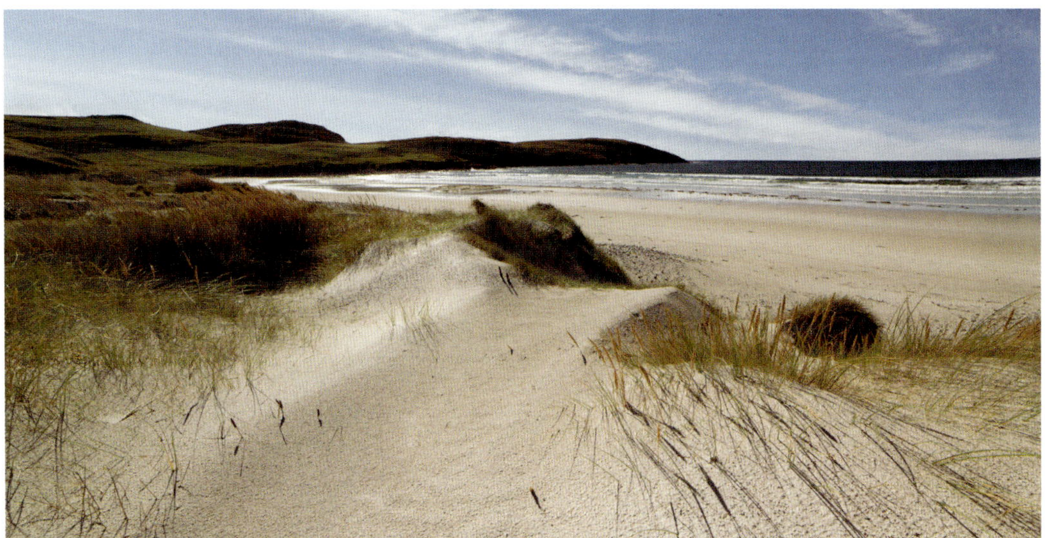

West Bay, Vatersay

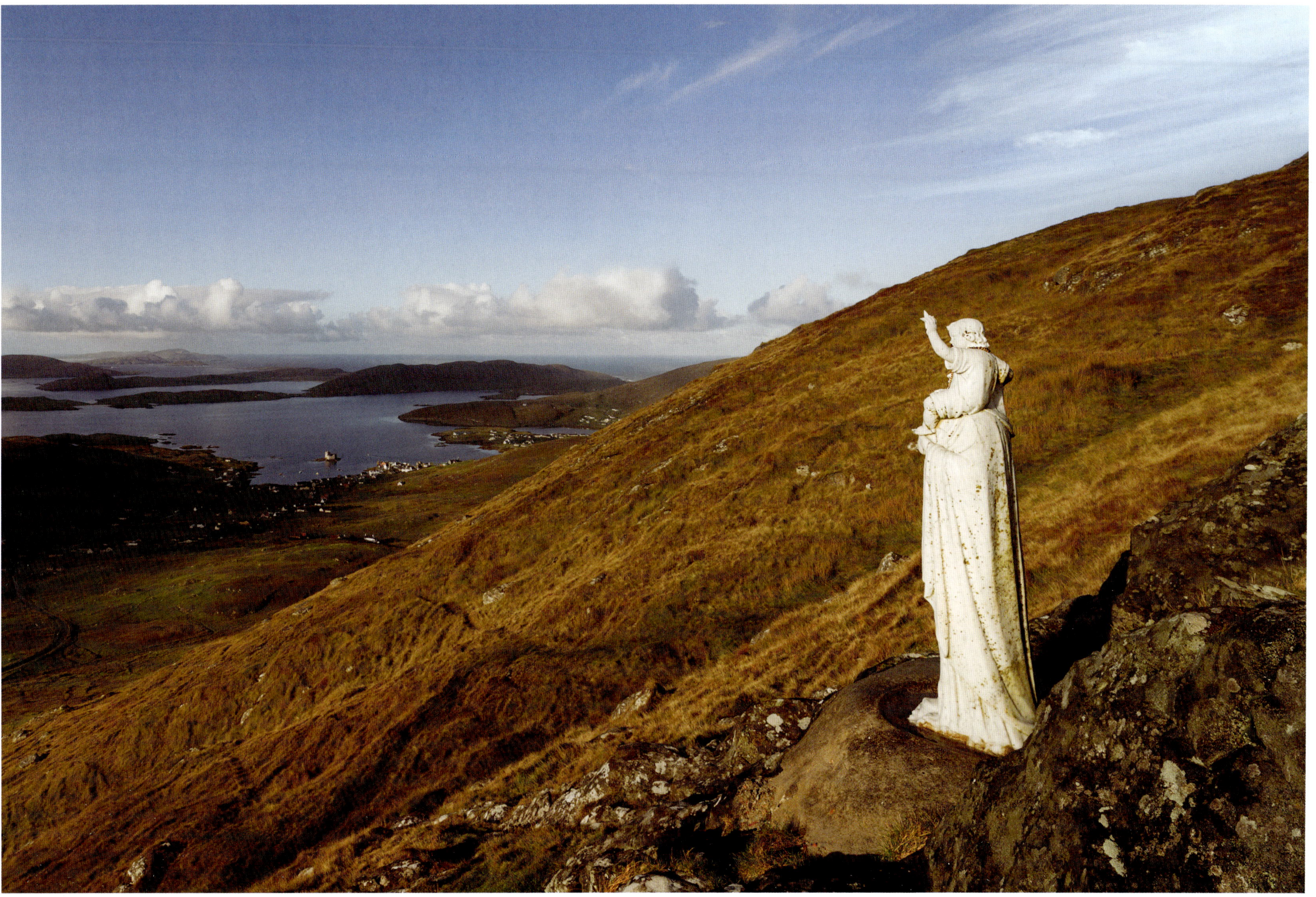

Brevig Standing Stone

A short climb up from the wooded grove at Cruachain is the Neolithic Brevig standing stone. It stands 3 metres tall and from down in the bay can easily be mistaken for a lone figure surveying the Sea of the Hebrides. A second 2.5-metre stone lies broken in two close by, with a third lying along the same alignment approximately 15 metres down the hill. To the south-west stands the shell of a derelict hut, further enhancing the sense of eerie abandonment.

The Neolithic period lasted from about 4,000 to 2,500 BC. During this period, the climate was a few degrees warmer than today and the local hunter-gatherers began to settle into small agricultural communities. With the development of early settlements came these mysterious monuments. Nobody can be certain of their purpose, but many believe they were used in conjunction with the sun, moon, and stars to mark the changing of the seasons. Understanding these transitions would have been important for these early farmers.

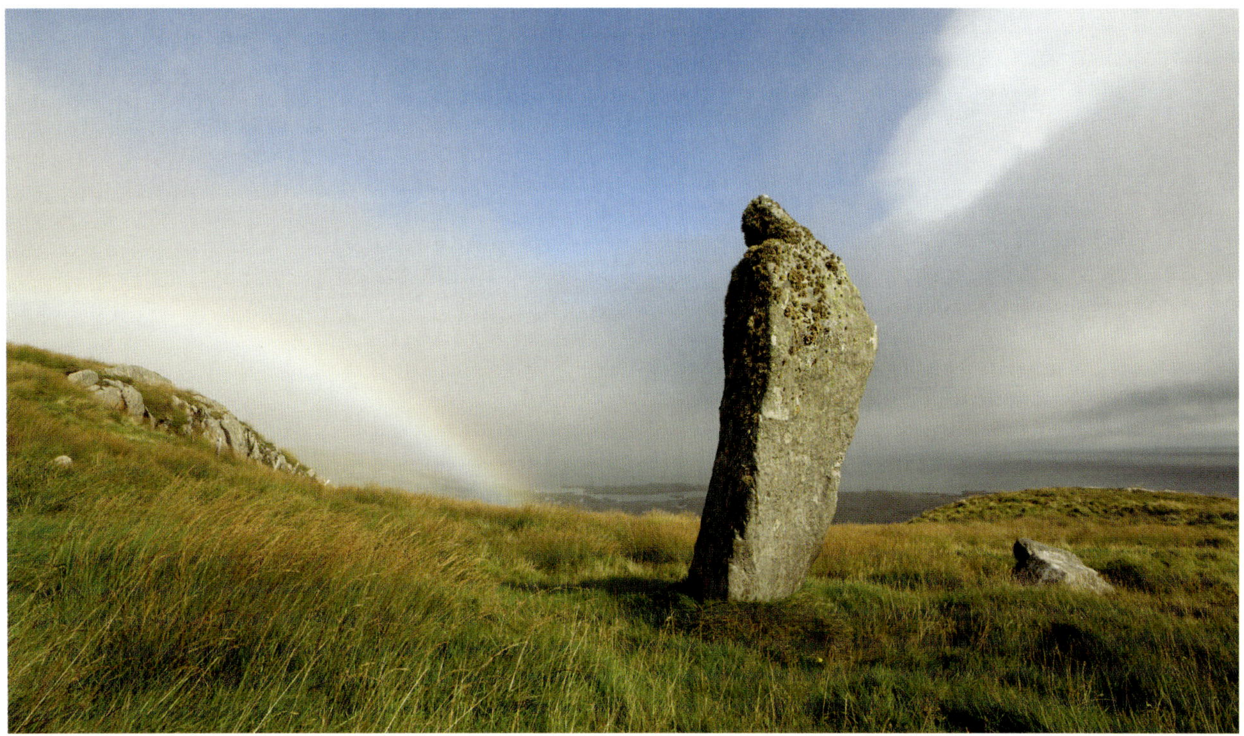

The largest surviving standing stone on the islands

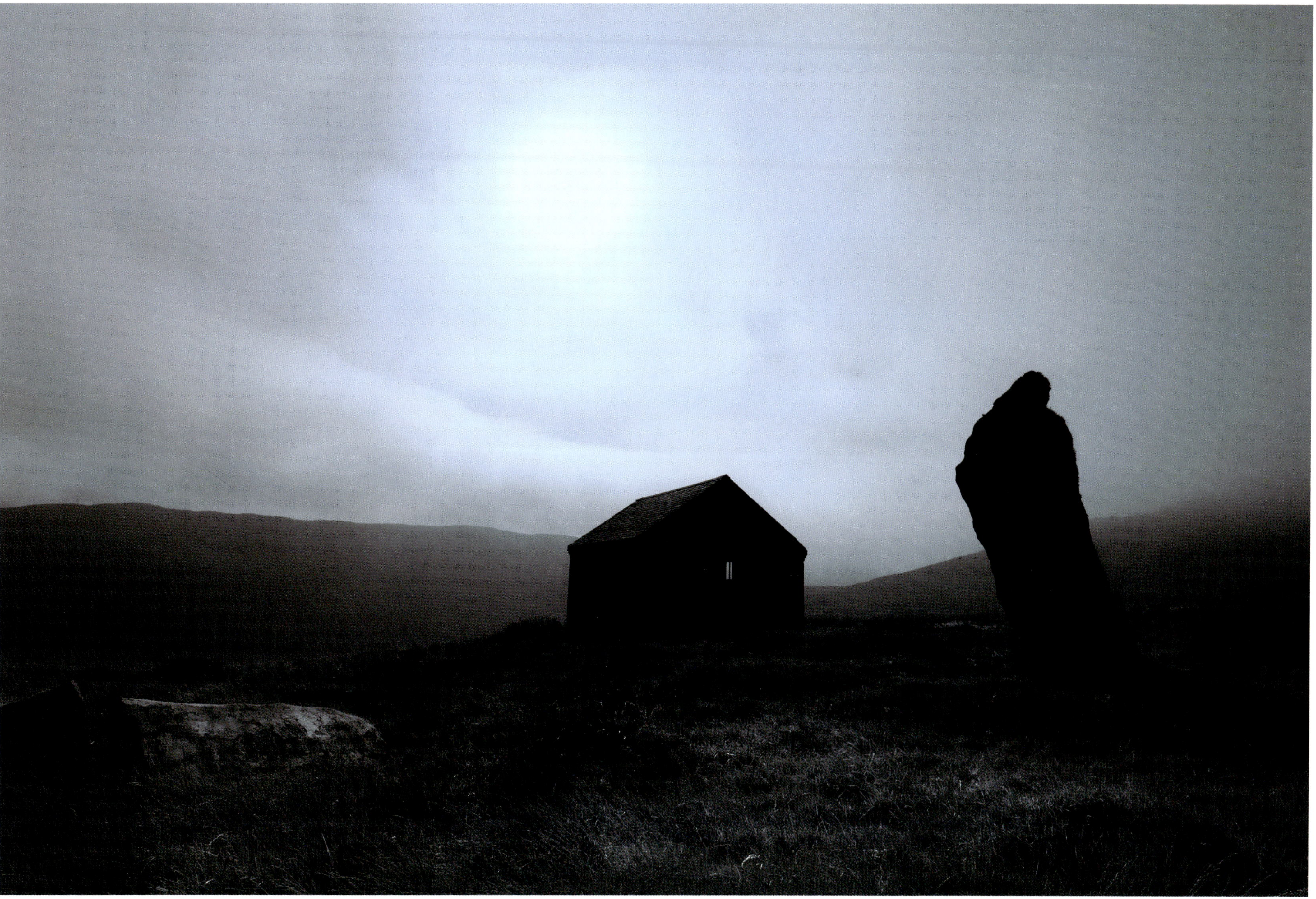

Cairns and Duns

To the trained eye, Barra and Vatersay present a dense tapestry of fascinating archaeological remains dating from pre-history through to the 19th century. Walkers exploring the valleys and hilltops may well stumble upon the vestiges of cairns and ancient forts, known locally as duns.

Just to the north of the Borve Valley is Dun Bharpa, the best-preserved chambered cairn in the Western Isles. Actually believed to be a Neolithic passage grave rather than a fort, Dun Bharpa is an impressive 30 metres long and 5 metres high. The Borve Valley itself is a treasure trove of archaic sites. Just 800 metres to the south-west of Dun Bharpa are the ruins of Balnacraig, yet another chambered cairn.

At Allt Easdal, on the southern slopes of Ben Tangaval, the excavation of a level platform built by early Neolithic pioneers has revealed human occupation dating back some 6,000 years. The building of this platform represented a substantial investment of energy and time and the site was continuously occupied for over 1,000 years. In the late 18th century it was settled on again as crofters (small-scale farmers) took advantage of their Neolithic predecessors' labours and built a traditional black house there.

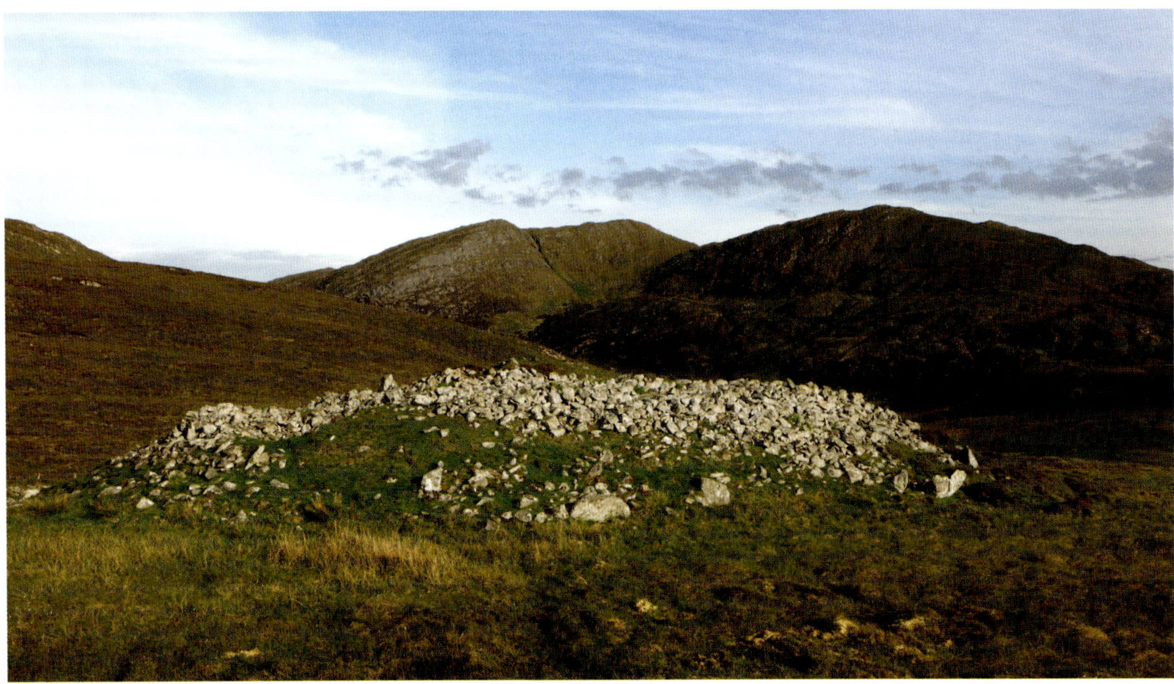

Dun Bharpa

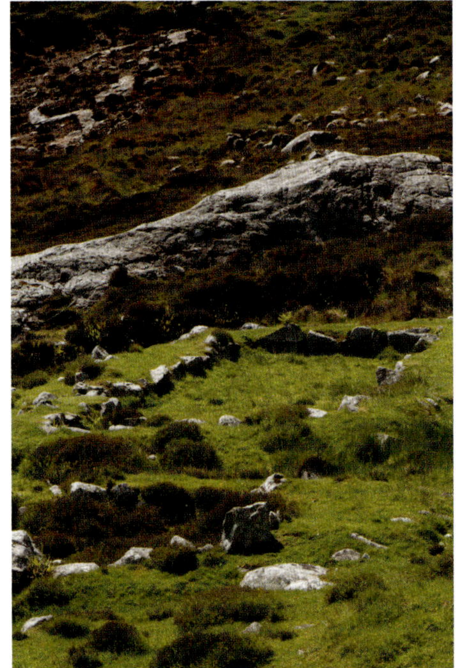

Allt Easdal

Right: Ruins of Balnacraig chambered cairn, Barra

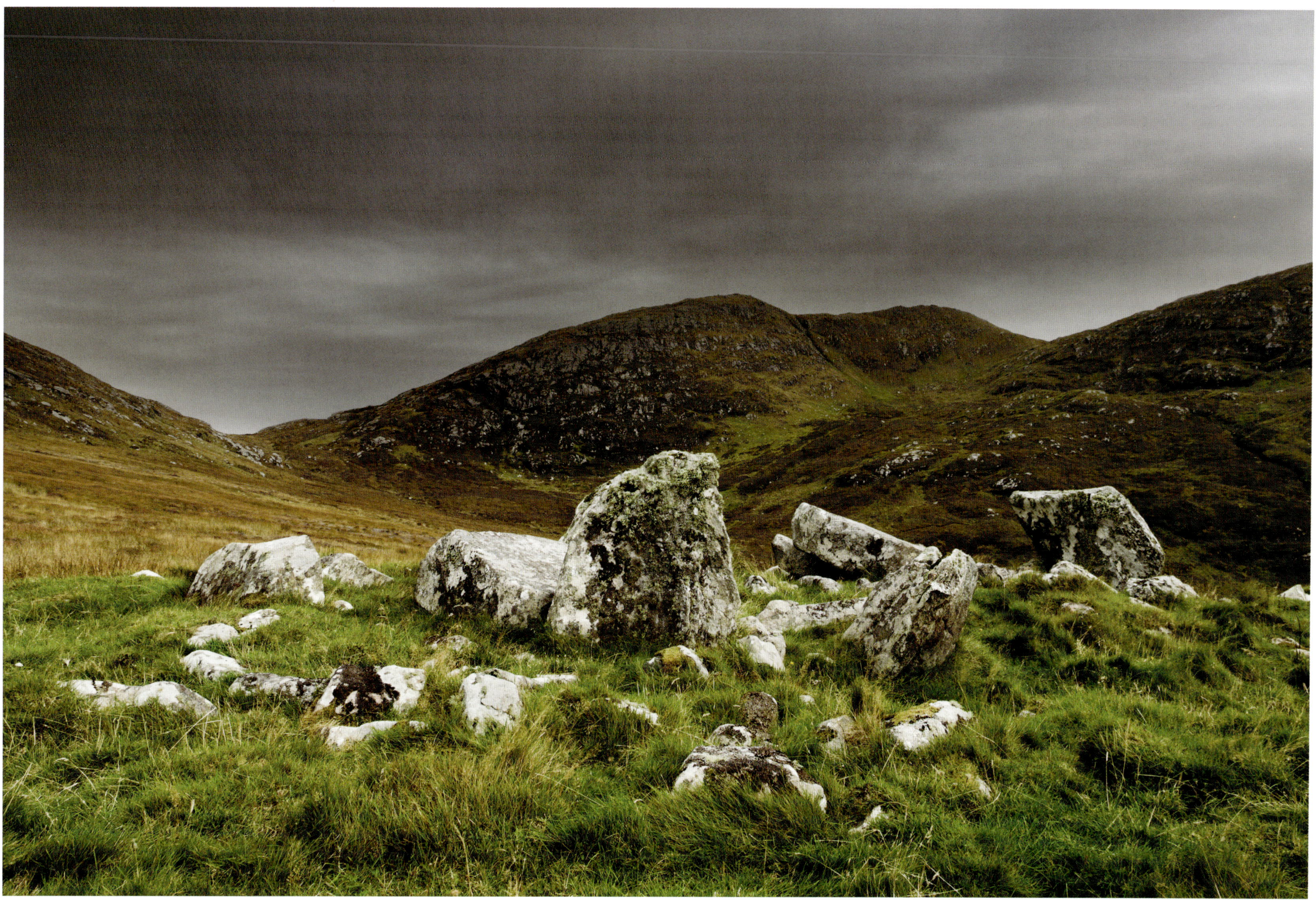

Loch Tangasdale

The enigmatic ruins of Macleod's Tower sit on an islet in Loch Tangasdale, also known as Loch St. Clair. This medieval refuge is believed to have been built in the mid-15th century over the remains of an Iron Age dun by John the Rough. John was the son of the notoriously brutal Marion of the Heads, so named for the many beheadings she ordered, including those of her two stepsons.

Originally three storeys high and with walls nearly a metre and a half thick, what remains today stands at about half that height. Brightly coloured lichens cover much of the ruins. Lichens are particularly sensitive to pollution so thrive in the clean air of the Hebrides. More than 500 species are found on the islands.

Loch Tangasdale is also known for its excellent fishing and is rated one of the best places in Scotland for brown trout. Rising from the southern shore is Ben Tangaval, which at 333 metres is the second highest peak on Barra.

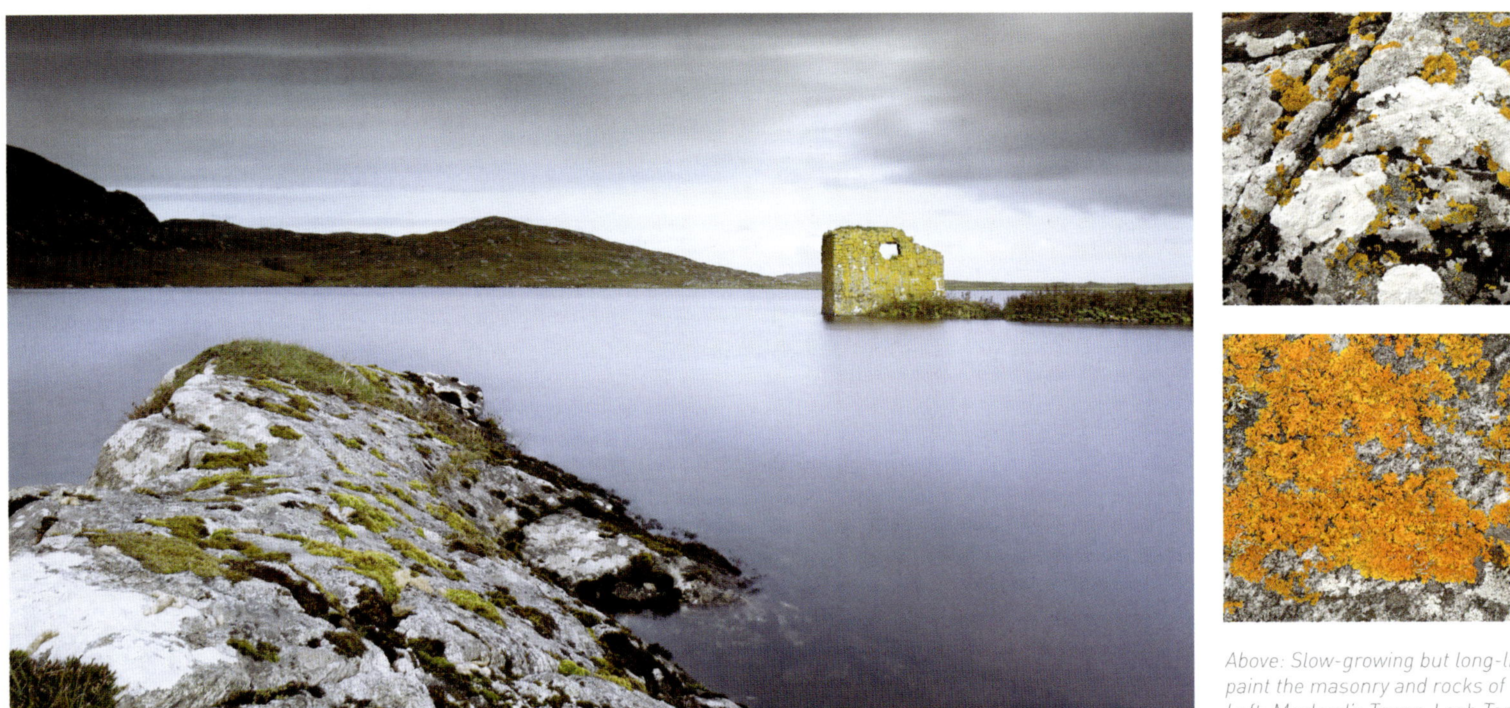

Above: Slow-growing but long-lived lichens paint the masonry and rocks of the Hebrides
Left: Macleod's Tower, Loch Tangasdale

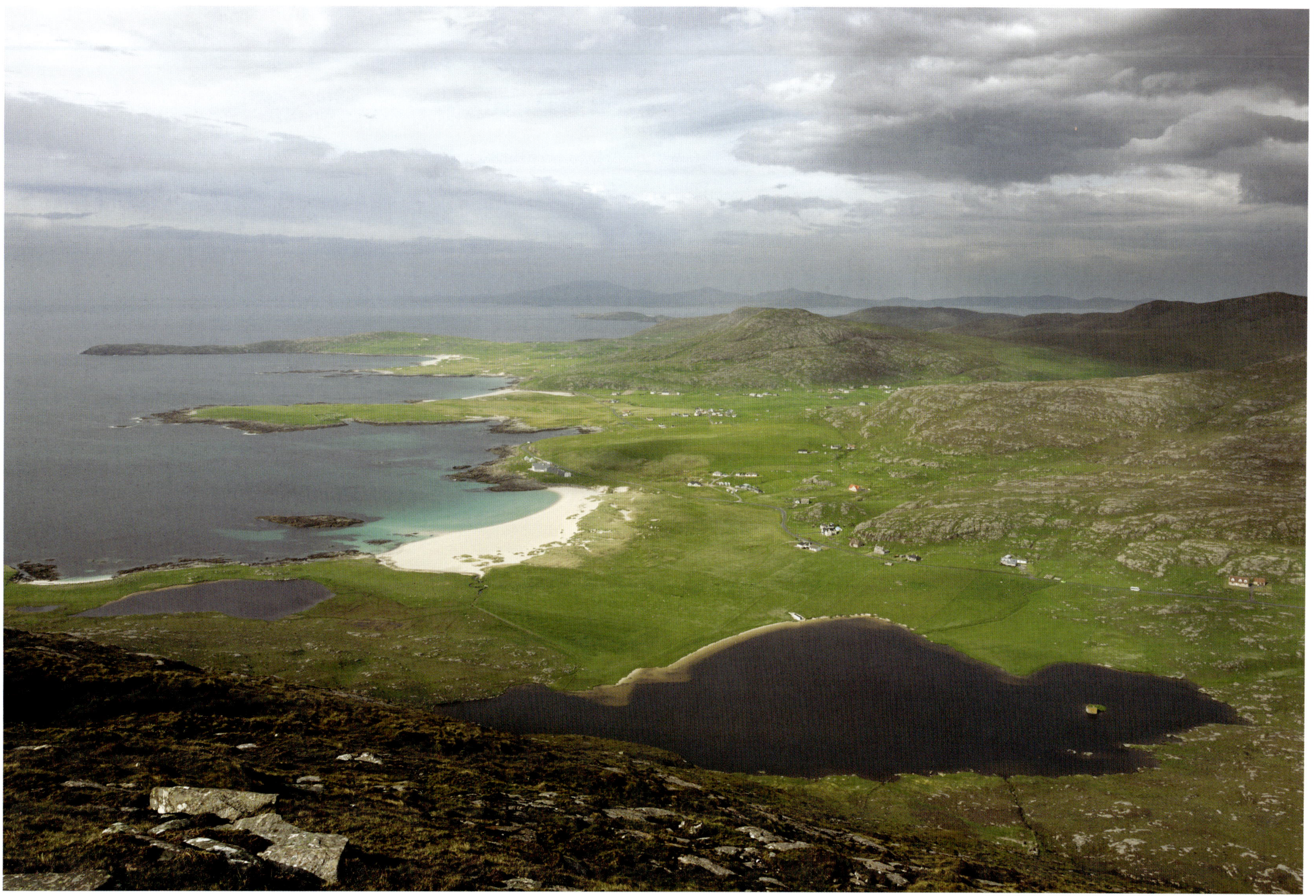

Castlebay

Castlebay is the largest settlement on Barra and takes its name from Kisimul Castle, located in its harbour. Castlebay's heyday was in the late 19th century, when it was a major centre for the herring trade. During the summer, up to 400 boats thronged the harbour and 24 piers bustled with gutters, coopers, curers, and foreign buyers. Standing over the village is the imposing Catholic church *Our Lady, Star of the Sea*, which opened in 1888 to serve the swelling population during the herring-trade boom.

Today the herring boats have gone, but Castlebay is still the island's main port. Most of the shops, as well as the only bank, can be found here. During summer the hotels, bars, and cafes are busy with tourists, who together with the fishing industry form the backbone of the island's economy.

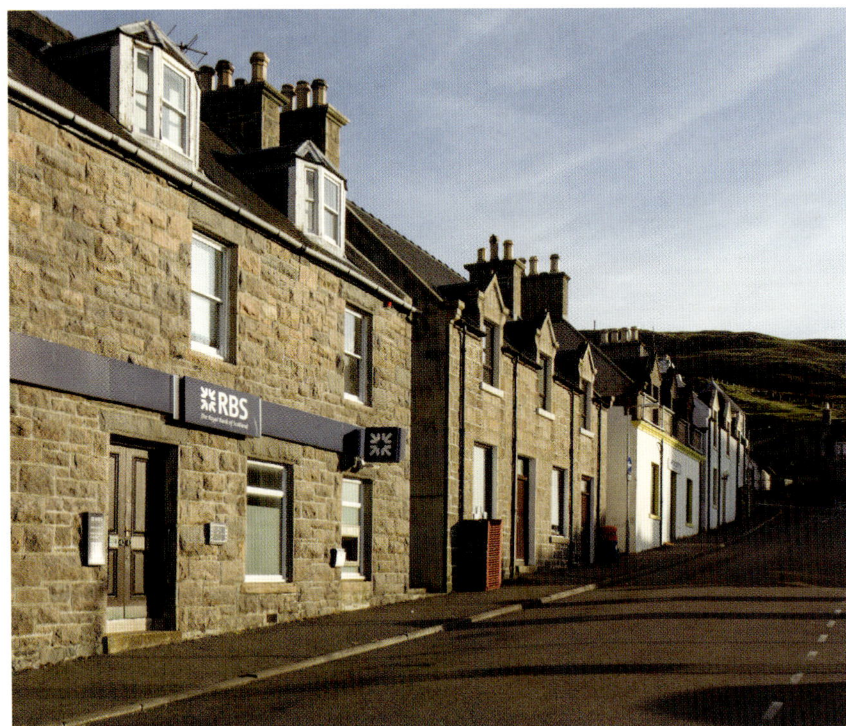

Above: Pier Road, Castlebay
Right: Castlebay from Vatersay
Overleaf: Castlebay from Heaval, Barra

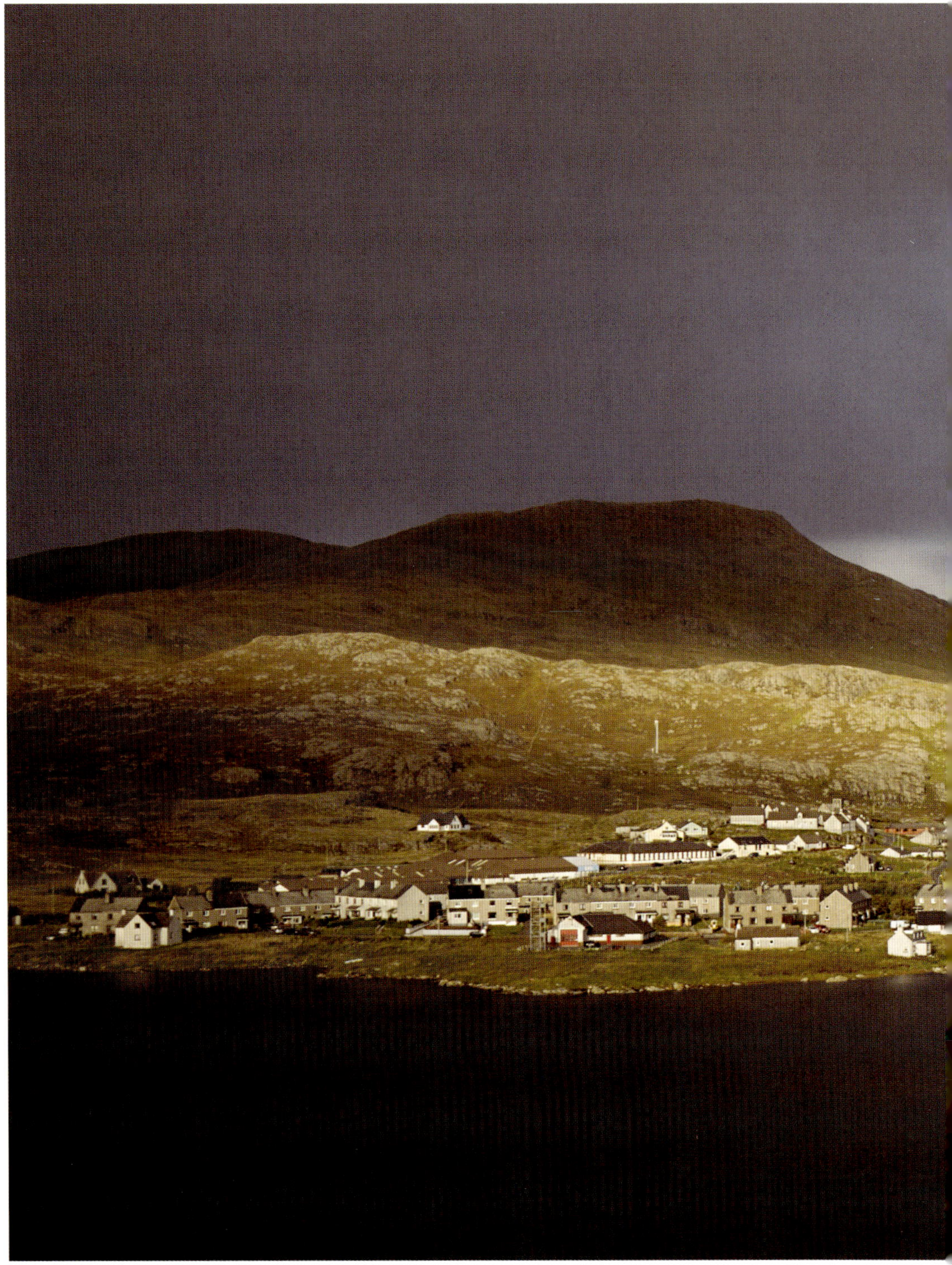

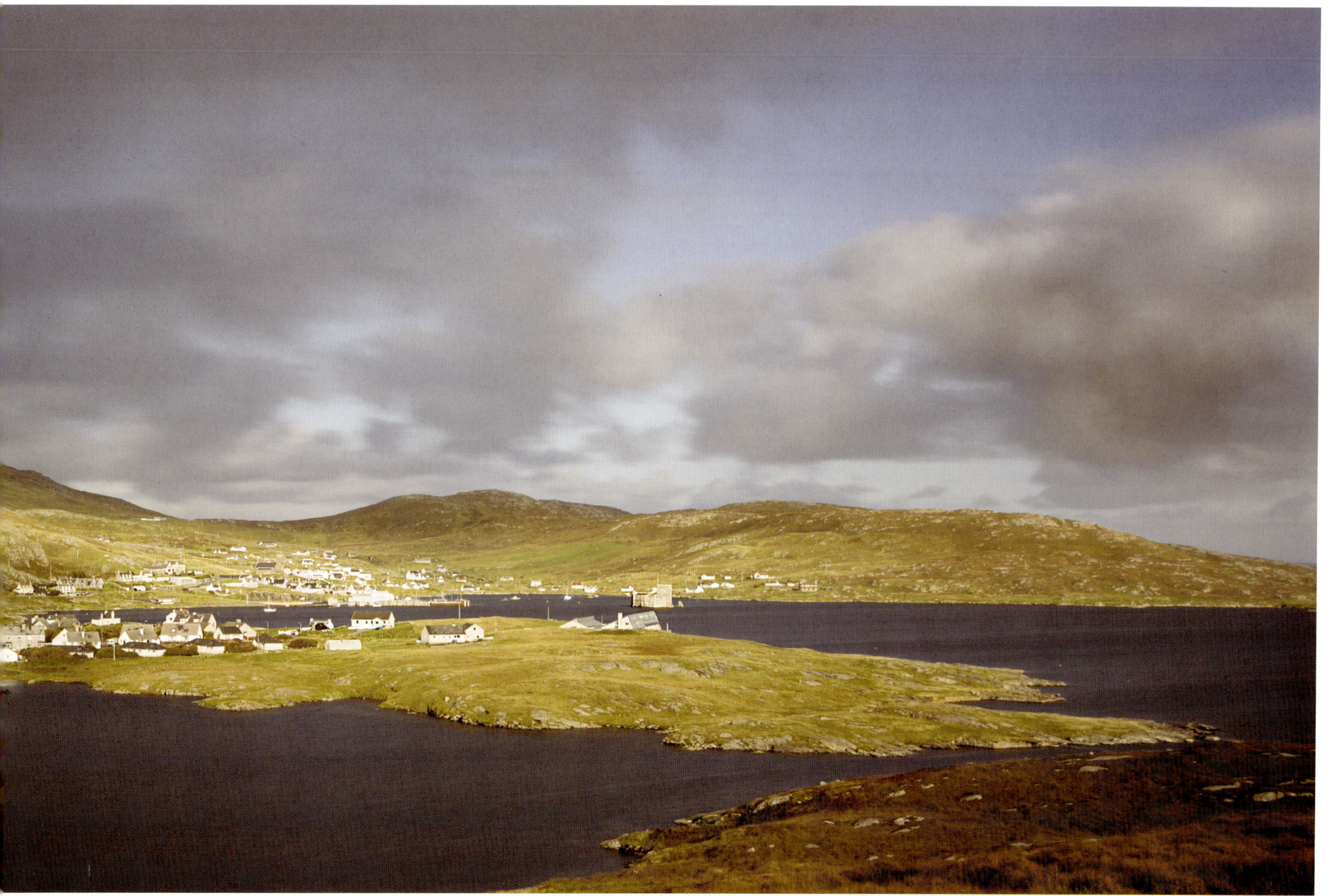

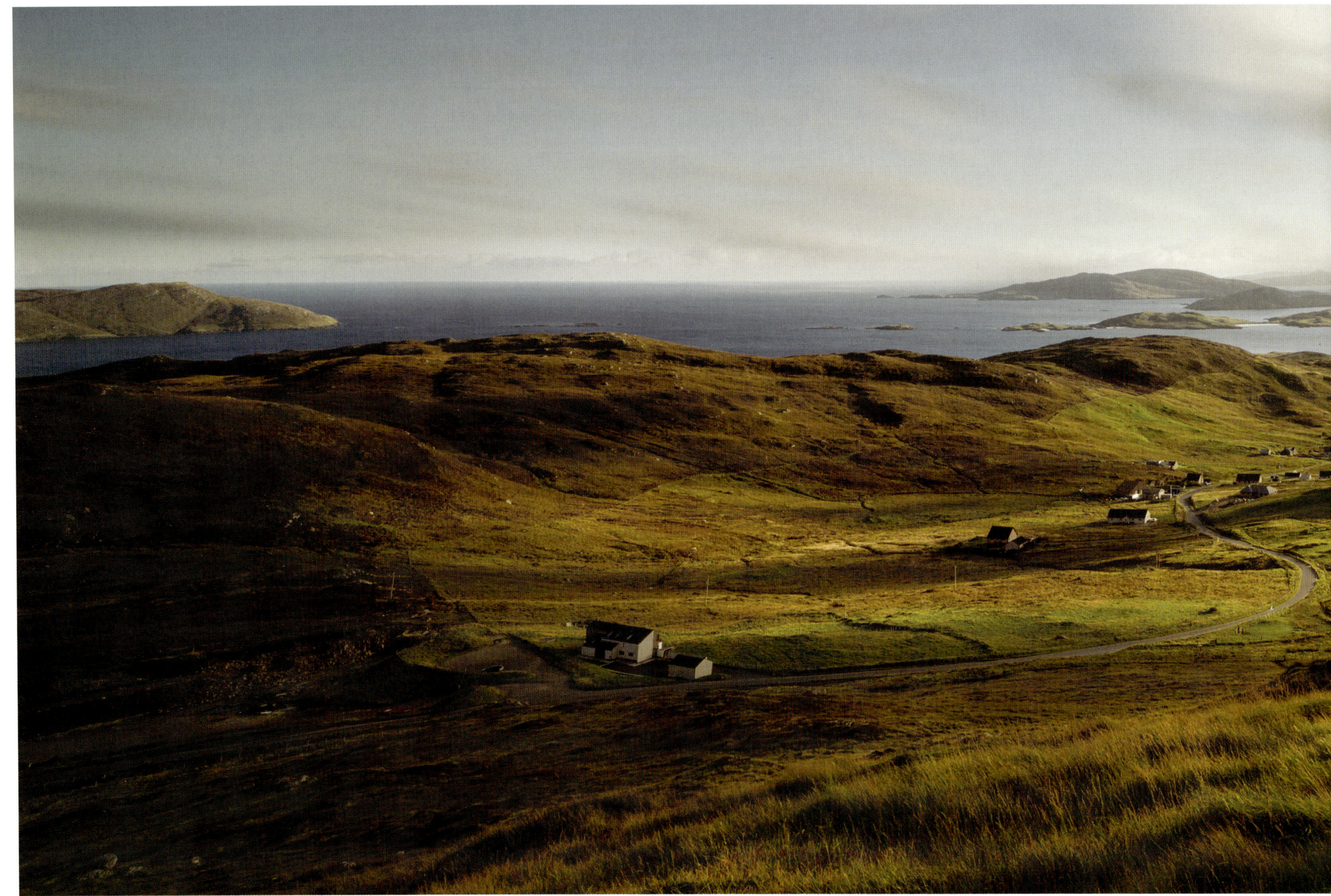

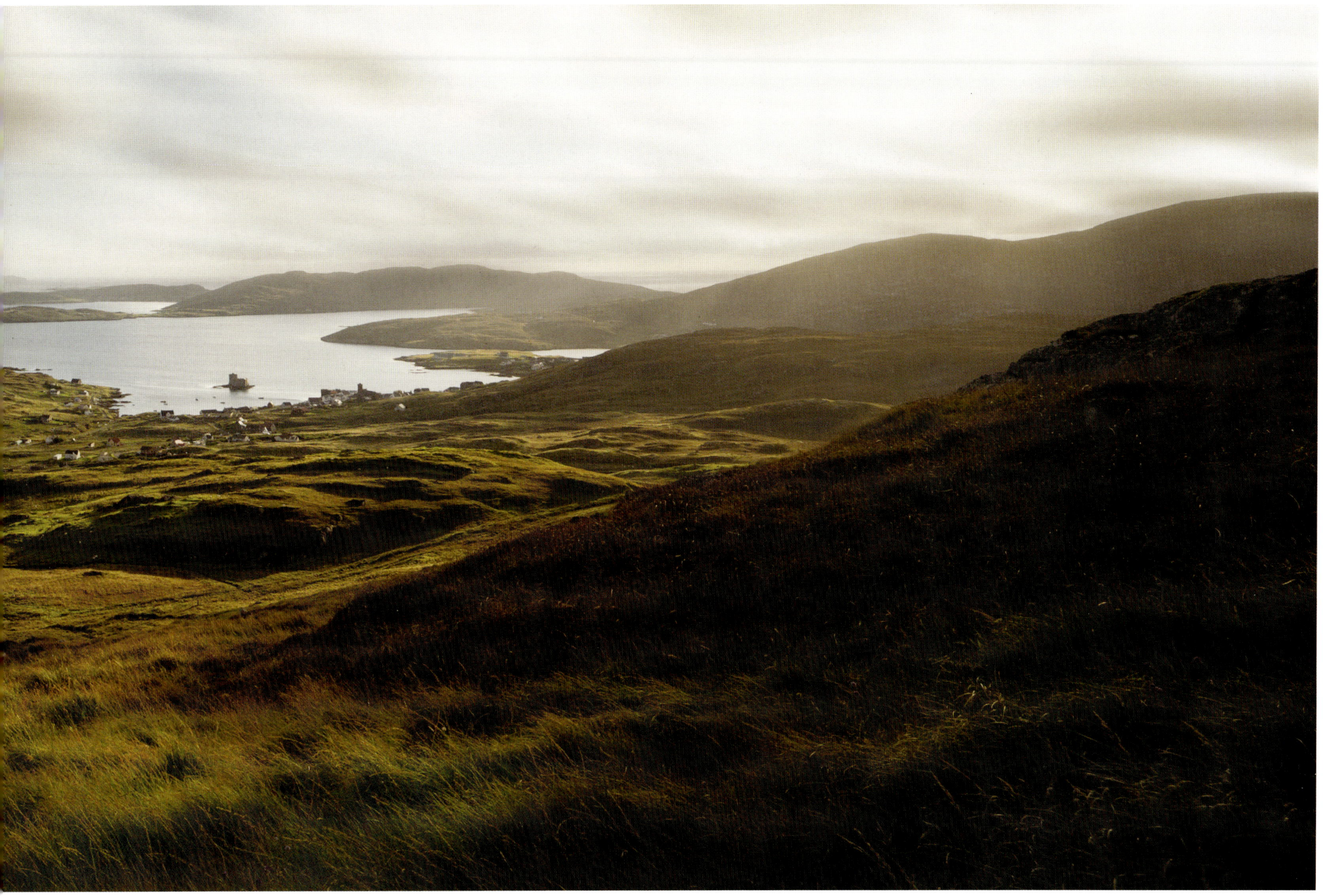

Cille Bharra

At the centre of the Eoligarry peninsula is Cille Bharra, dedicated to the 7th-century Irish monk St Barr, after whom Barra is believed to be named. Within its stone walls are three chapels, two of which are now in ruins. The remaining North Chapel has been substantially renovated and houses a replica of the nationally significant Kilbar Stone, a rare example of combined Christian and Viking symbols. The stone has a carved cross on the front, and on the reverse side, Norse runes declare: *'This cross has been raised in memory of Thorgeth, daughter of Steinar.'* The original cross, which stood in the churchyard, has been moved to National Museums Scotland in Edinburgh for safekeeping.

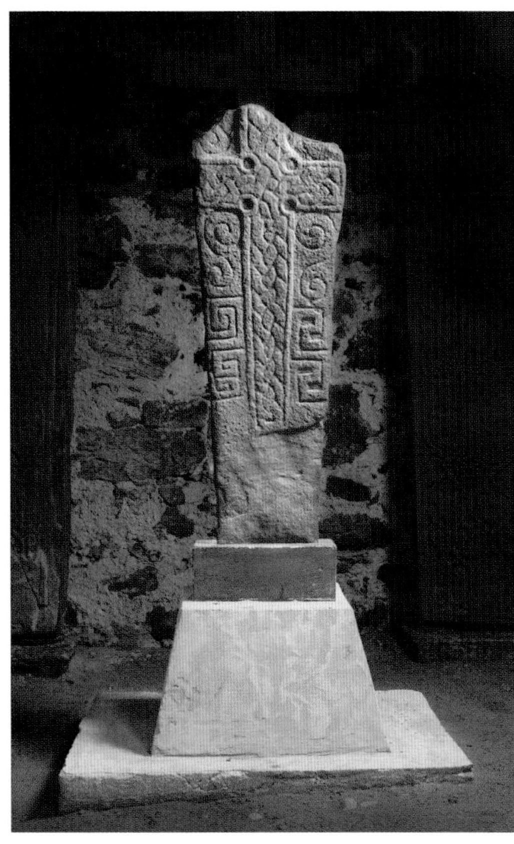

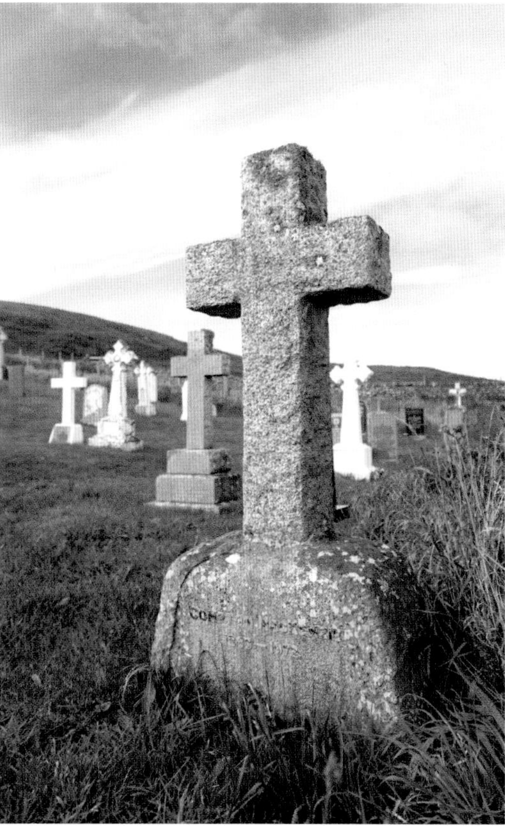

Cille Bharra's other claim to fame is the grave of novelist Sir Compton Mackenzie, author of *Whisky Galore* (1947). The book is based on the true story of the SS *Politician* running aground in 1941 on nearby Eriskay, with an estimated 250,000 bottles of whisky on board. It depicts the canny islanders' efforts to keep some 'liberated' cargo from the authorities. The SS *Politician* was also carrying banknotes worth several million pounds in today's currency, much of which has never been accounted for.

Mackenzie's popular tale was adapted for the screen and filmed on Barra, with many islanders starring as extras.

Right: The replica of the Kilbar Stone
Left: Sir Compton Mackenzie's gravestone

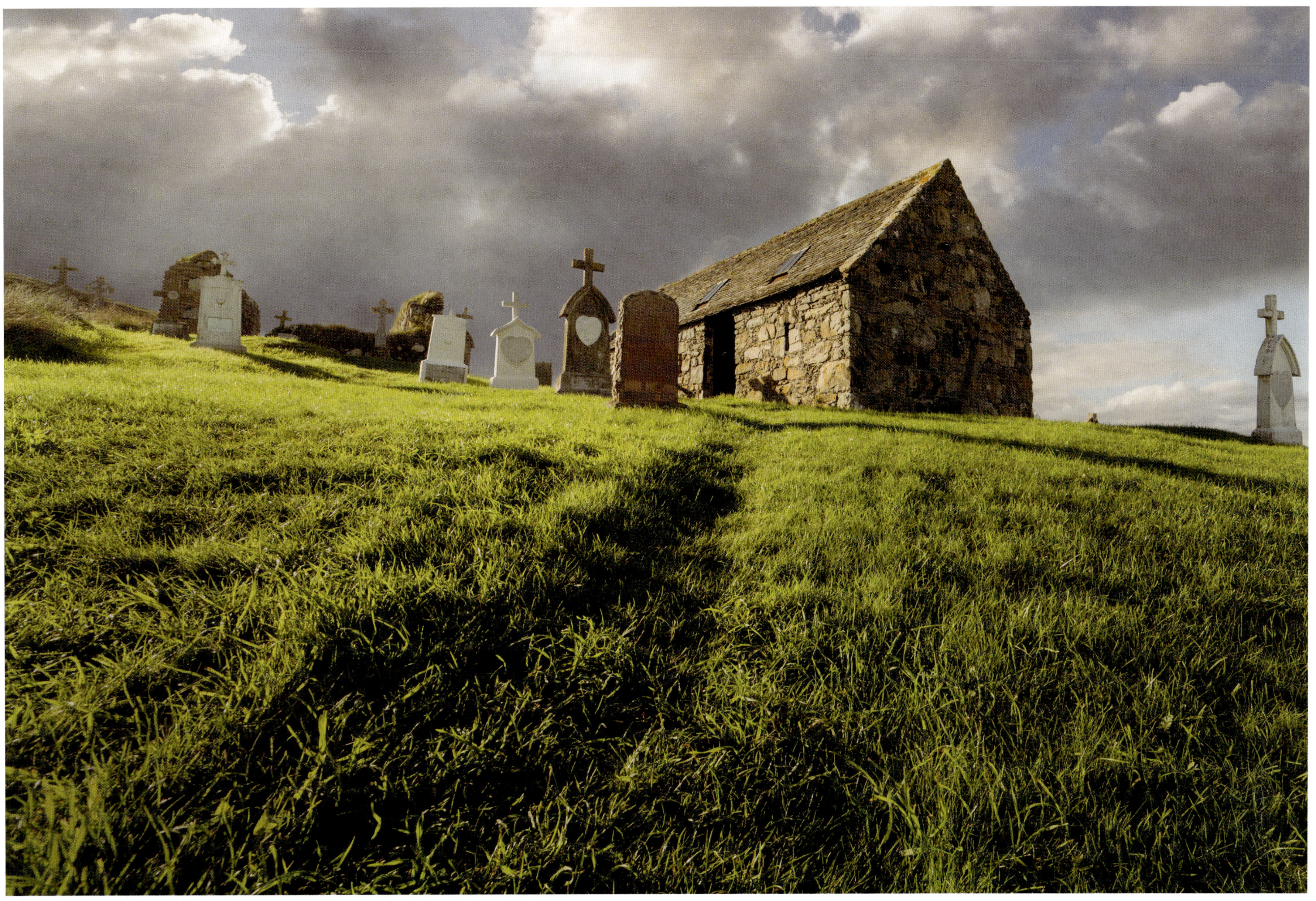

Western Rock

Much of the character of the Western Isles derives from its ice-scoured, rocky landscape. The Outer Hebrides' geology consists largely of metamorphosed granite, known in Scotland as Lewisian gneiss. Originating from volcanic material, Lewisian gneiss is the oldest rock in the British Isles and among the most ancient in the world, dating back 2,800 billion years. Over 1,500 billion years (about one third of the Earth's history), the original rock became deeply buried by continental movements and was subjected to extreme heat and pressure. Remelted and recrystallised, it was later thrust back to the surface bearing the telltale signs of its turbulent past. It is often beautifully veined, with pale grey to pink bands of quartz and feldspar crystals, and darker bands of amphiboles.

These predominantly treeless islands offer little else than rock in the way of building materials. Despite being extremely hard and difficult to work, Lewisian gneiss has been used to build everything from Neolithic dwellings and monuments through to the crofters' cottages still in use today.

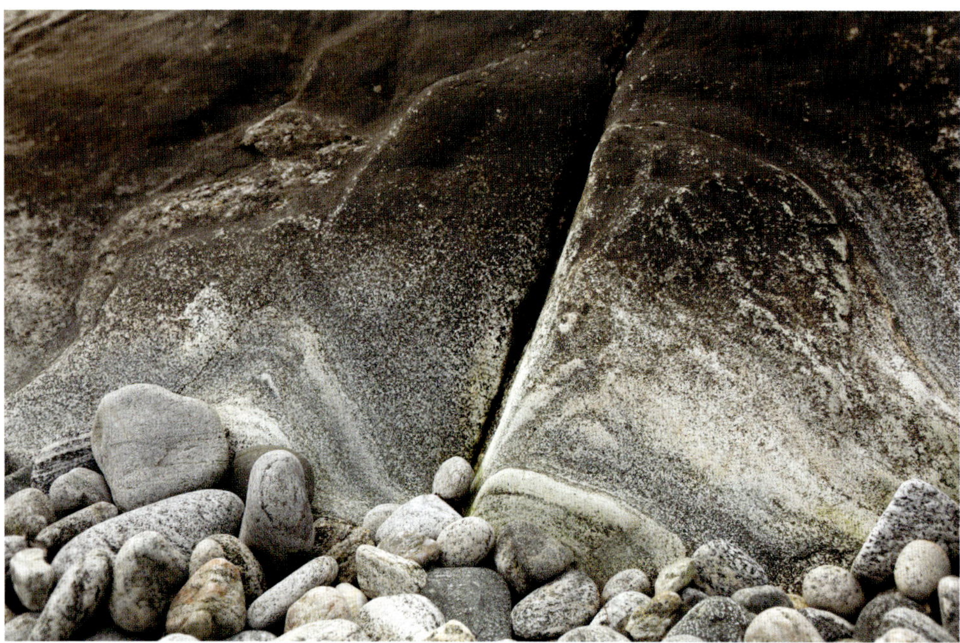

Beach pebbles stacked up against a boulder of banded granite

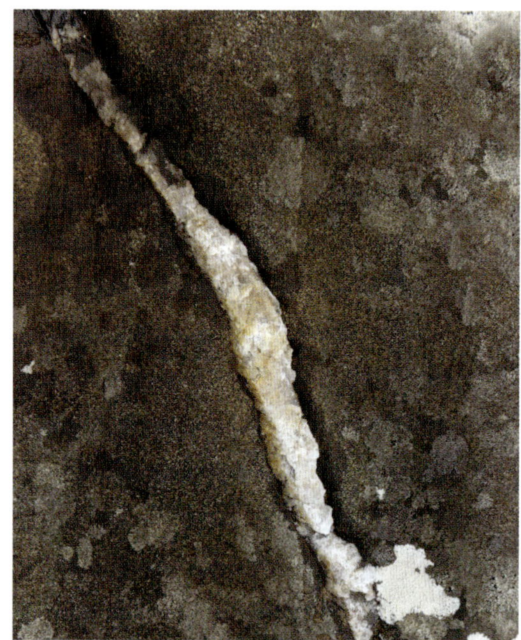

Crystal seam

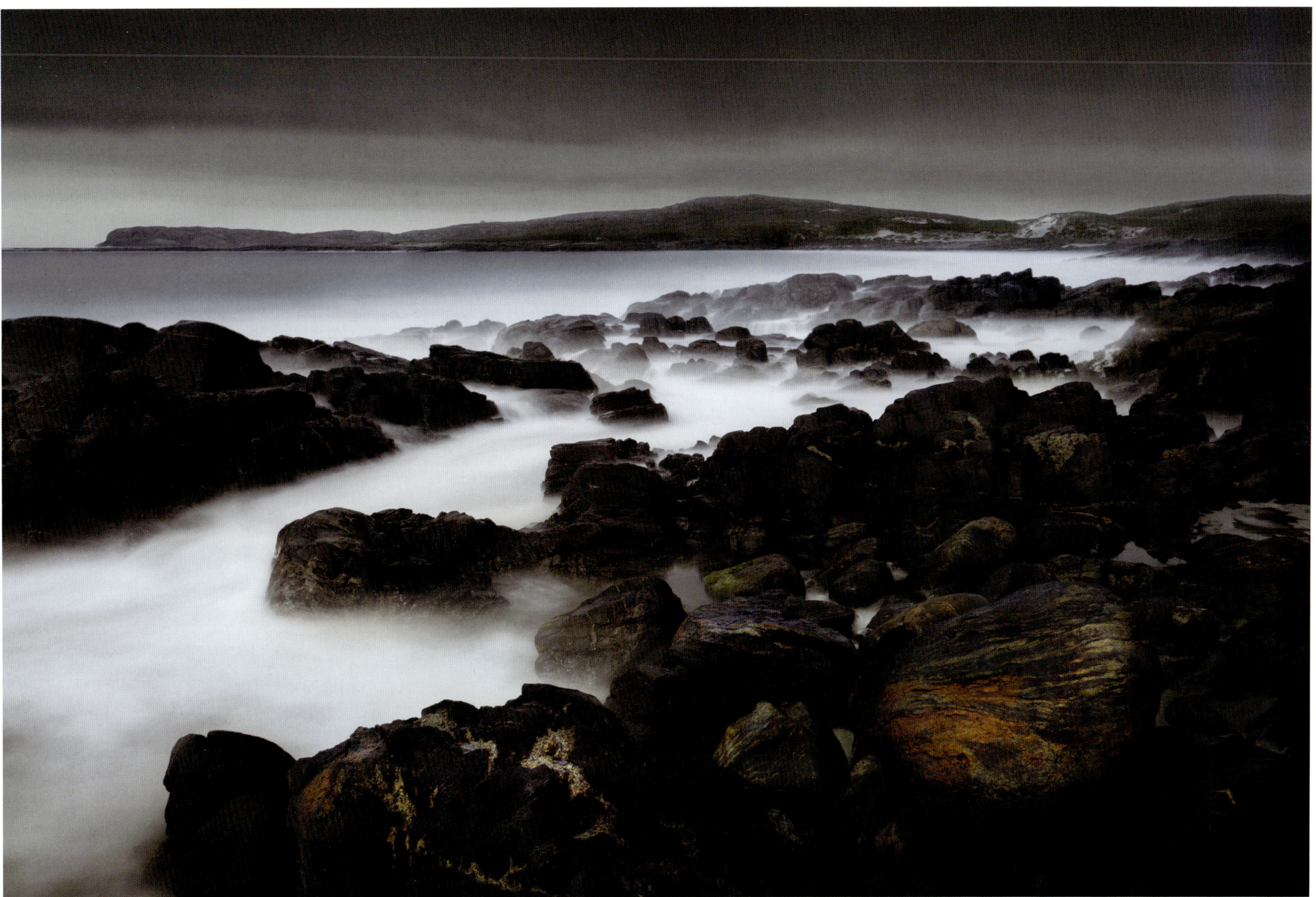

Ebb and Flow

For many islanders, the twice-daily ebb and flow of the tides has more relevance than Greenwich Mean Time. On rocky shorelines, the sea level can drop by up to 4 metres, revealing a complex and colourful world of marine flora and fauna, each organism adapted to tolerate the severe conditions of its own niche in the intertidal zone.

Here, algae and animals must endure twice-daily flooding, pounding surf, large fluctuations in temperature, and exposure to both sea and fresh water. As if that weren't enough, dehydration and starvation are also risks since most intertidal animals are able to feed only when submerged.

Like the algae and animals that have evolved to cope with these extremes, the islanders too have adapted. They have long taken advantage of the low tide to gather seaweed and molluscs. Kelp for fertiliser, soda, potash, iodine, and alginates used to be an important source of income, until the duty on imported kelp was removed in 1822 and the industry largely collapsed. More recently, kelp has been put forward as a possible biofuel.

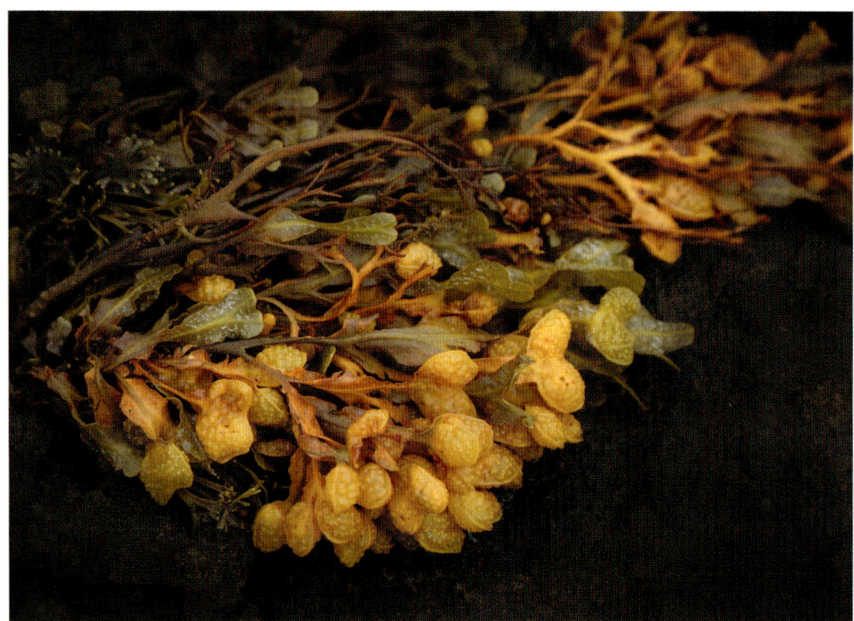

Seaweed cluster anchored to the rock

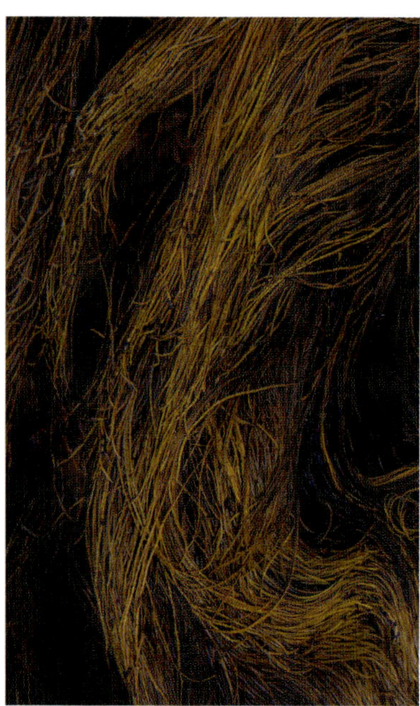

Edible thongweed

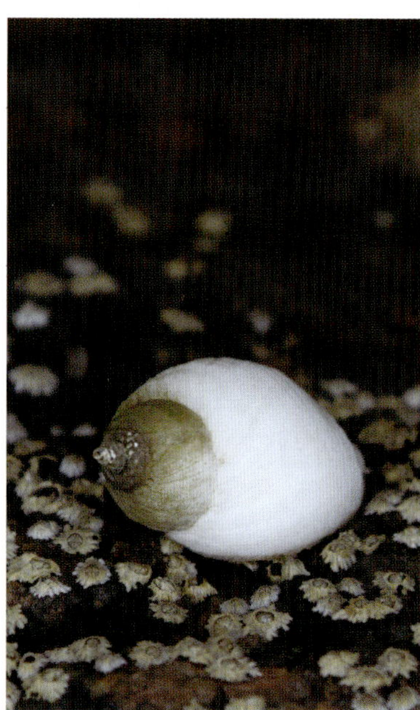

Periwinkle

Right: Low tide at Leanish Point, Barra

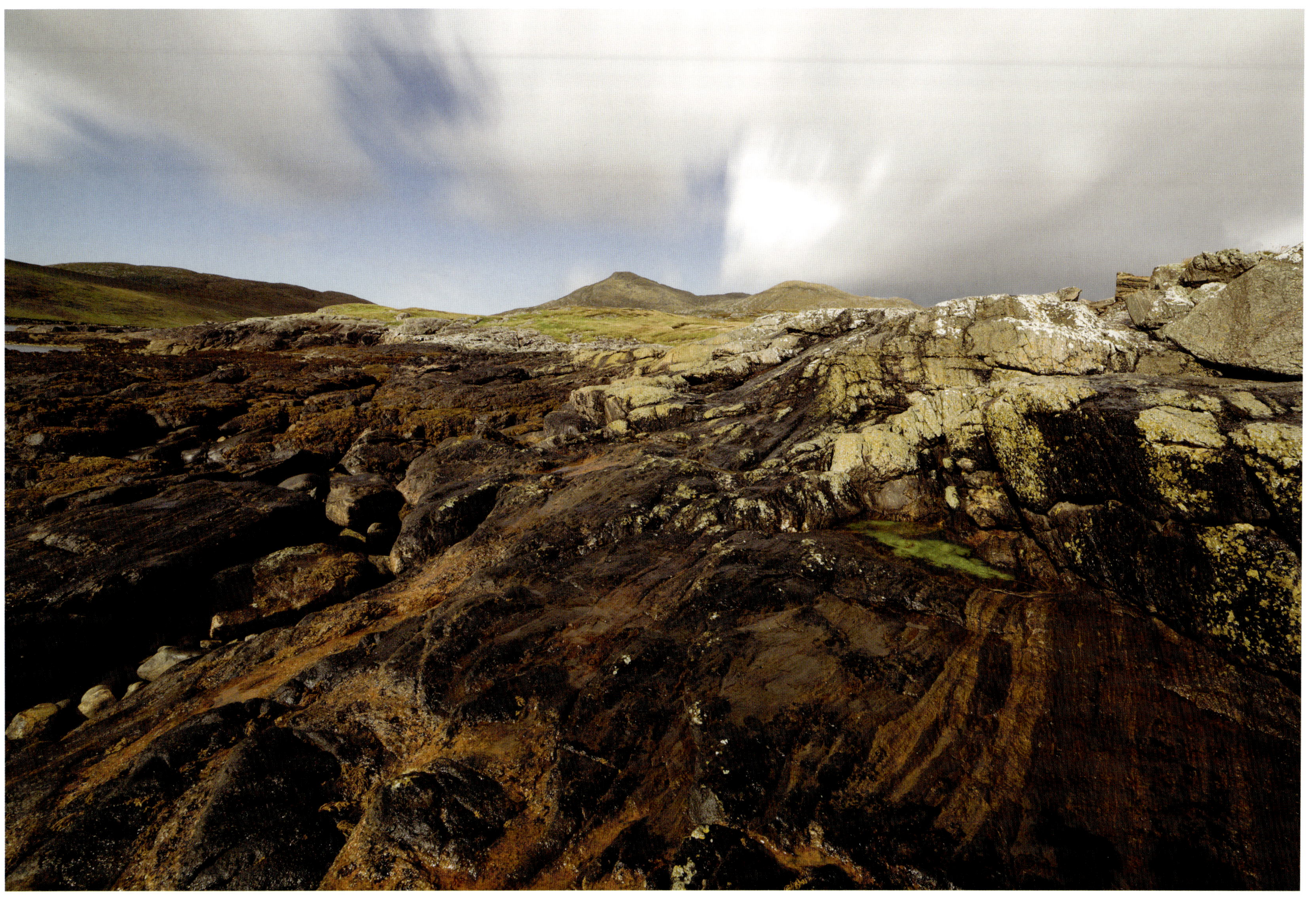

The Atlantic Coast

Barra's western seaboard is renowned for its white-sand beaches, turquoise waters, and crashing surf, which have earned the island the tongue-in-cheek moniker 'Barrabados'. There are five beaches from which to choose, starting in the south with the steeply sloping Tangasdale, and concluding in the north with the spectacular, mile-long stretch of Tràigh Eais. The frequently huge Atlantic rollers and relatively warm Gulf Stream waters have made Barra's west coast a Mecca for anglers and beachcombers. In more recent times, they have also been attracting adventurous surfers looking for new breaks.

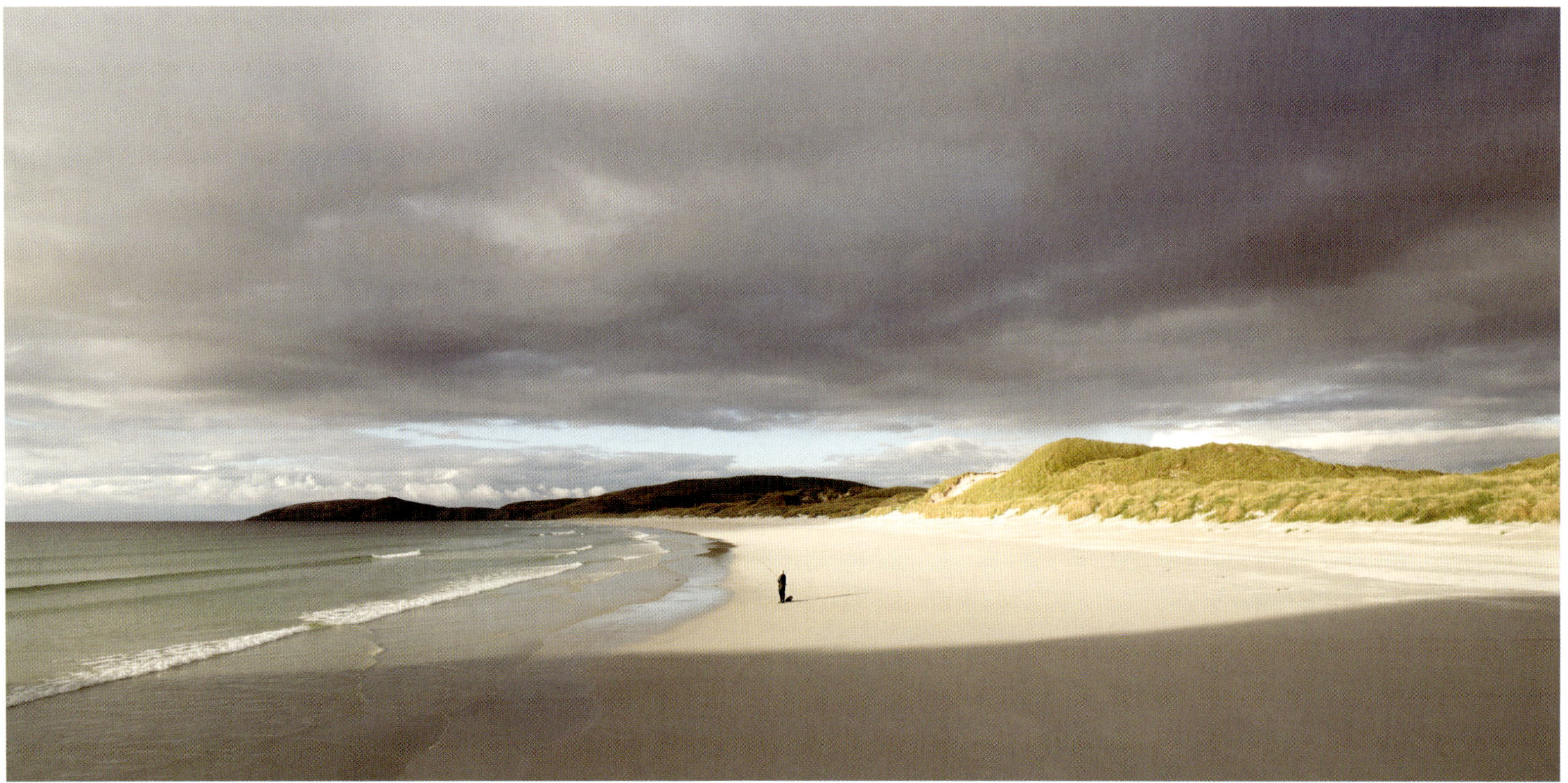

Surf-casting on the west coast

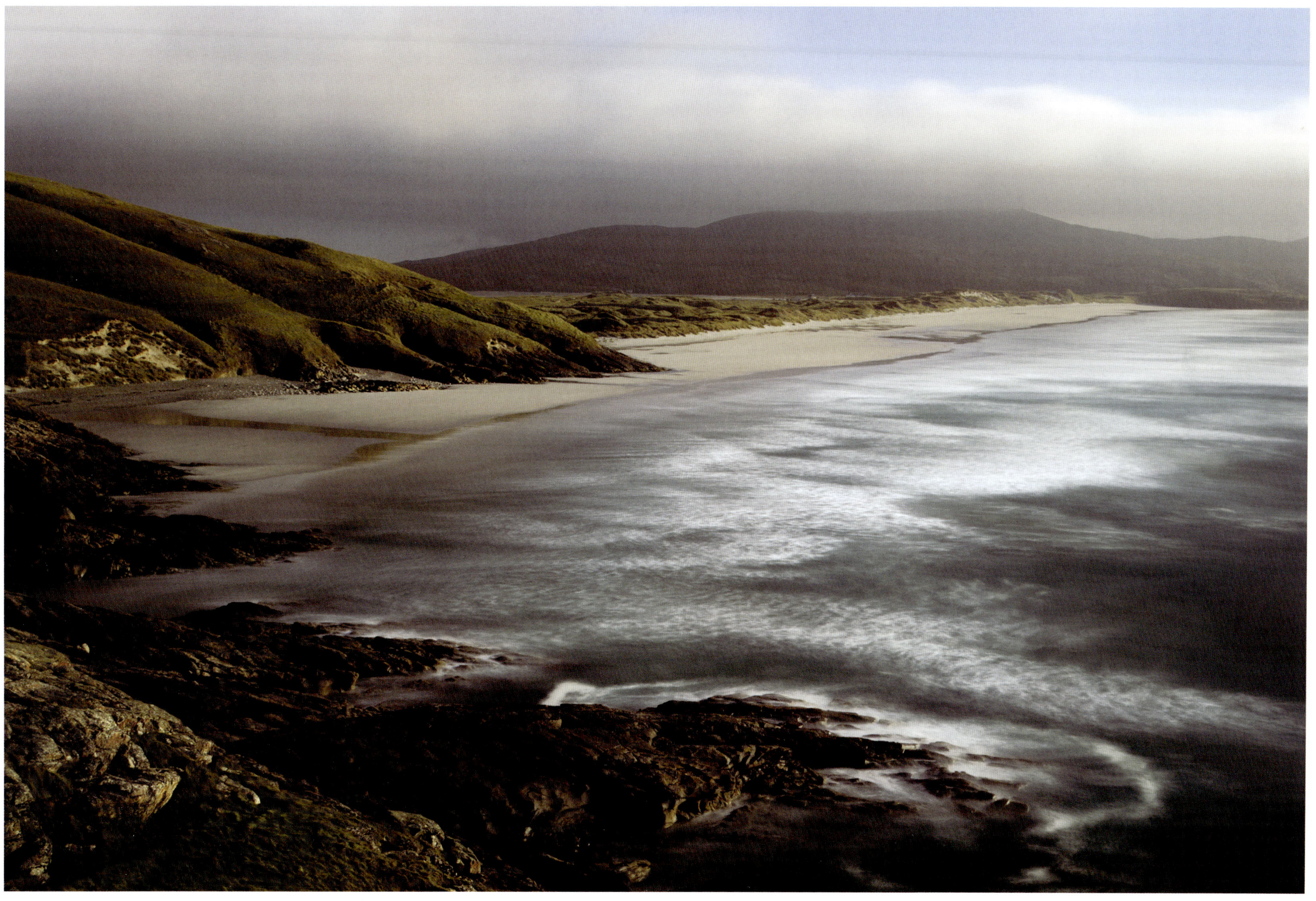

Vatersay Sands

Vatersay's bays offer a choice of stunning white-sand beaches. On the east and overlooked by the old schoolhouse is the gently sloping and comparatively sheltered Vatersay Bay. A low strip of dunes and machair separates it from the wilds of West Bay on the Atlantic side. At the northern end of the isthmus lie the victims of the *Annie Jane* sinking, buried in a mass grave as no wood was available for coffins.

Around the coast are a number of smaller, picturesque bays, each with it's own distinct character. On a clear day, South Bay offers views over to the Isle of Sandray. Abandoned by people in 1934, Sandray is now a haven for seabirds.

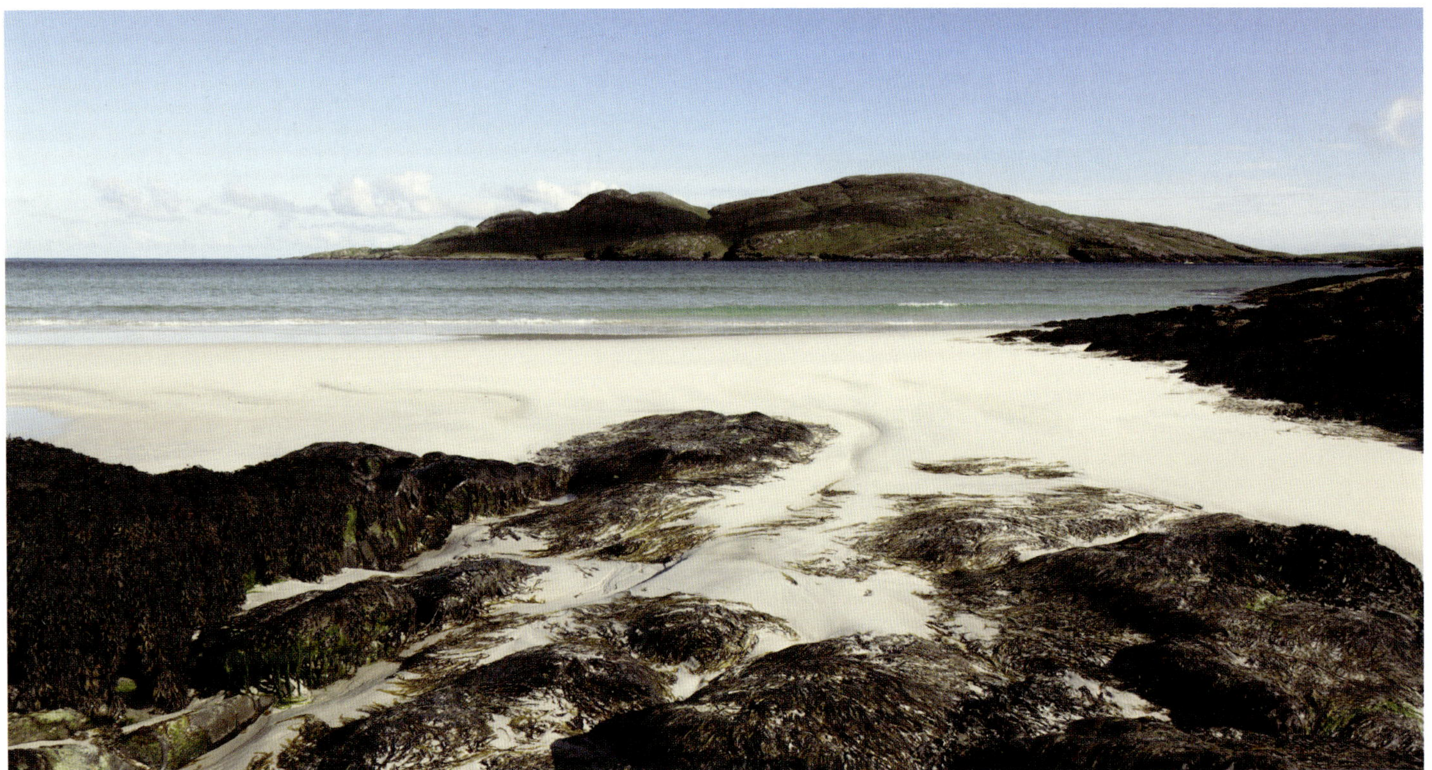

South Bay, looking towards Sandray

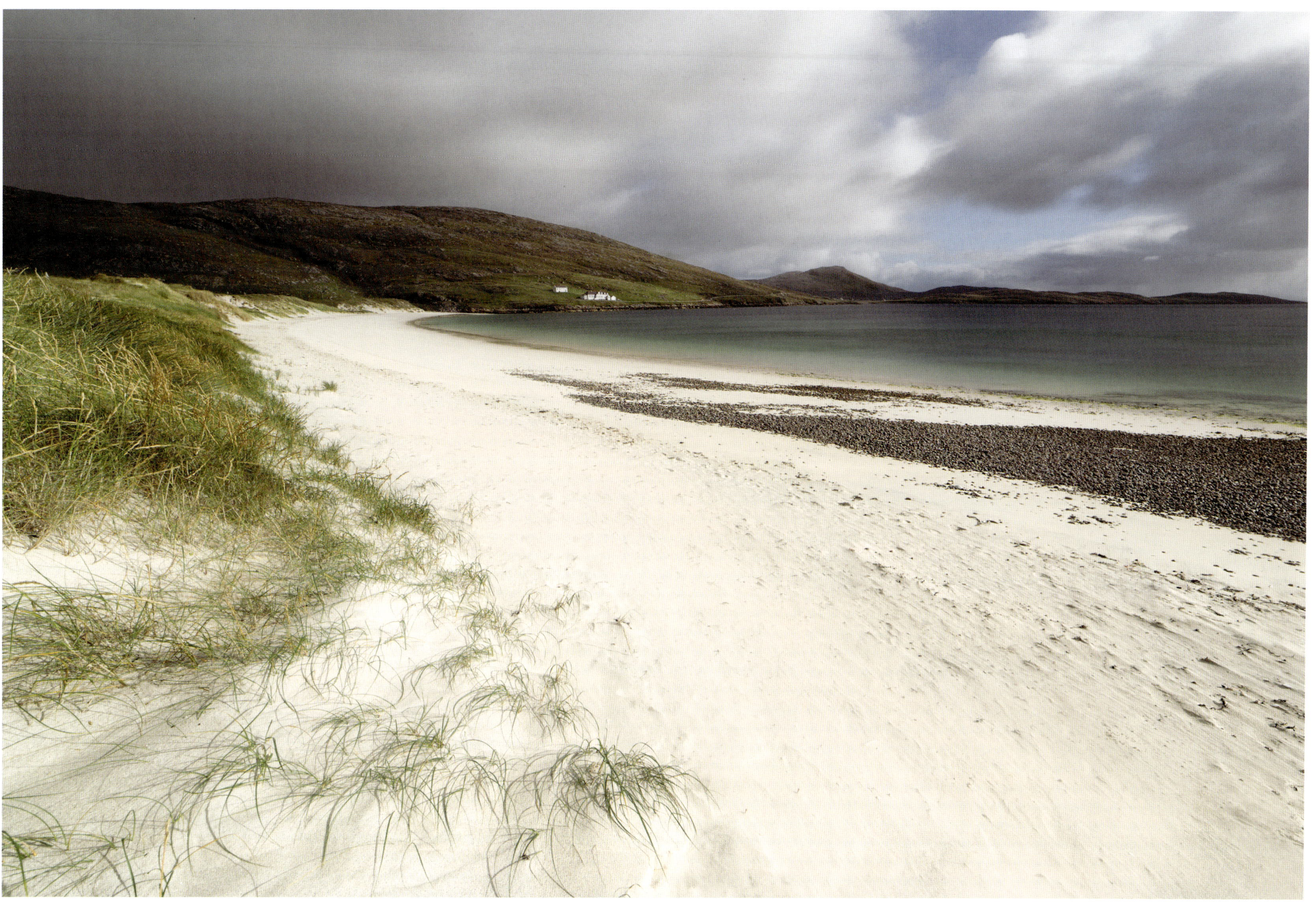

The Bounty of the Sea

Seamanship and fishing are in the blood of Hebrideans, who have long harvested the rich waters that encircle their island homes. From the heady days of the herring boom in the late 19th century through to the modern operations of today, fisheries have played a crucial role in the local economy.

In recent times, balancing the industry's needs with the wider concern of conserving rare and important marine habitats has proved controversial. In 2013, the Sound of Barra, a stretch of shallow water between the north coast of Barra and the Isle of Eriskay, was designated a Special Area of Conservation (SAC). Established to protect harbour seal, reefs and sandbanks, including what is potentially the largest maerl (coral like algae) bed in the UK, it is hoped that this SAC will help boost tourism.

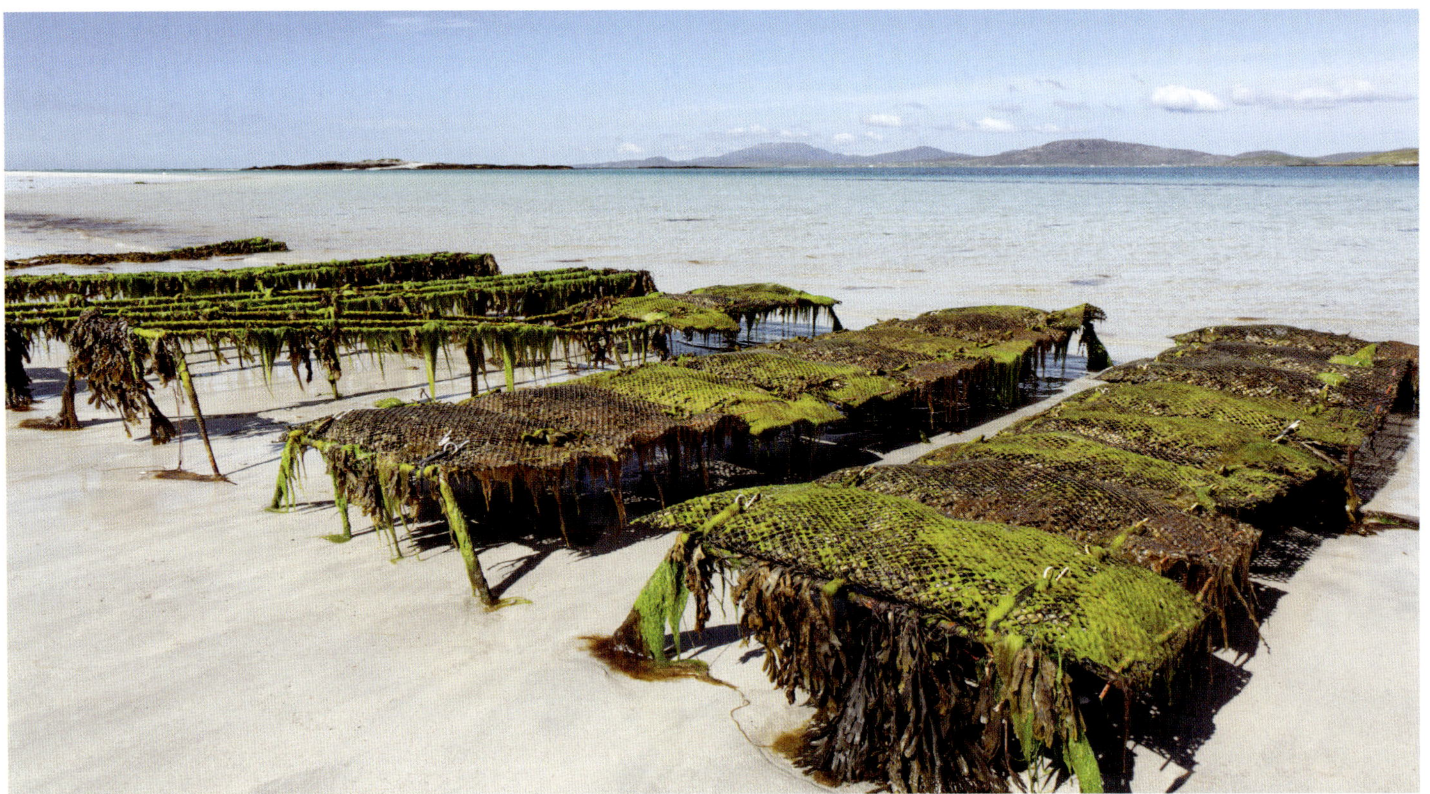

Oyster beds, Tràigh Sgùrabhal, Barra

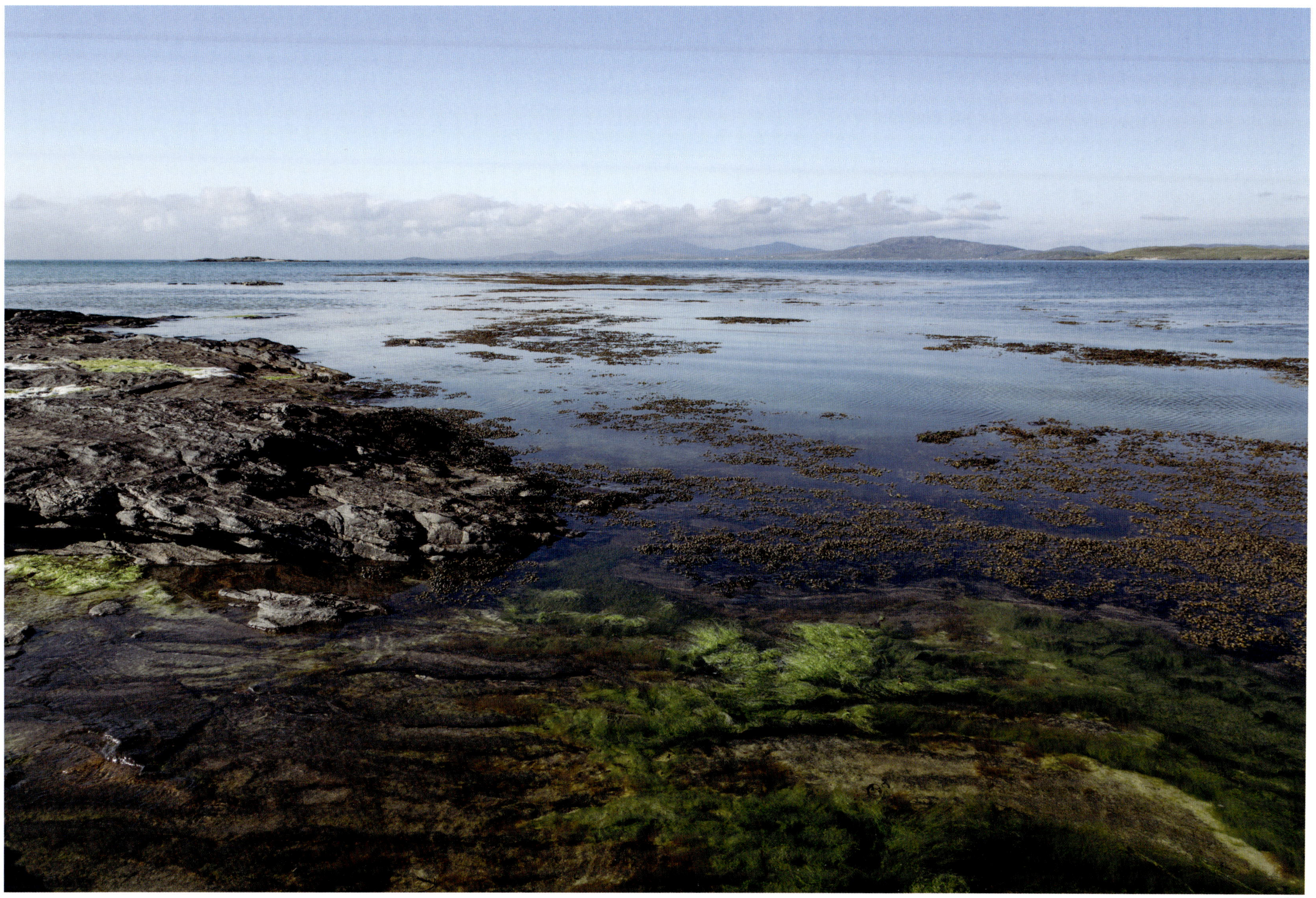

High and Dry

Hauled from the water for the last time, battered old fishing boats lie marooned on the rocks, or list awkwardly on grassy banks close to the shore. Symbols of the rugged Hebridean lifestyle, these salt-blasted hulks often find one final purpose as storage for fishing gear.

Fishing for crab and lobster with creels goes back generations and is still an important source of food and income today. The seas around Barra and Vatersay are also known for outstanding langoustine and scallops, as well as a host of white-fish species such as pollock, ling, and cod.

On Vatersay, conservation and recycling neatly come together, with bent and broken creels being strung across the dunes in an effort to slow the relentless erosion.

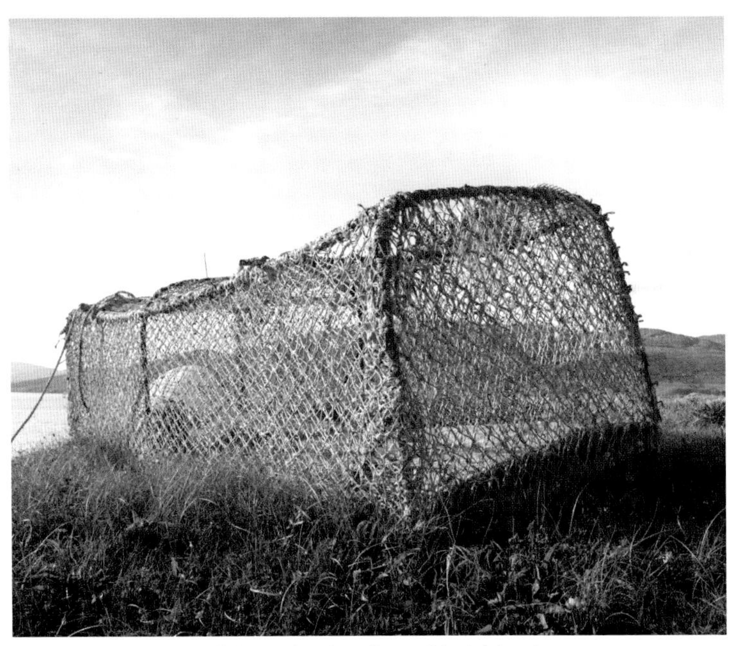

Creels are a common sight on the shorelines of both islands

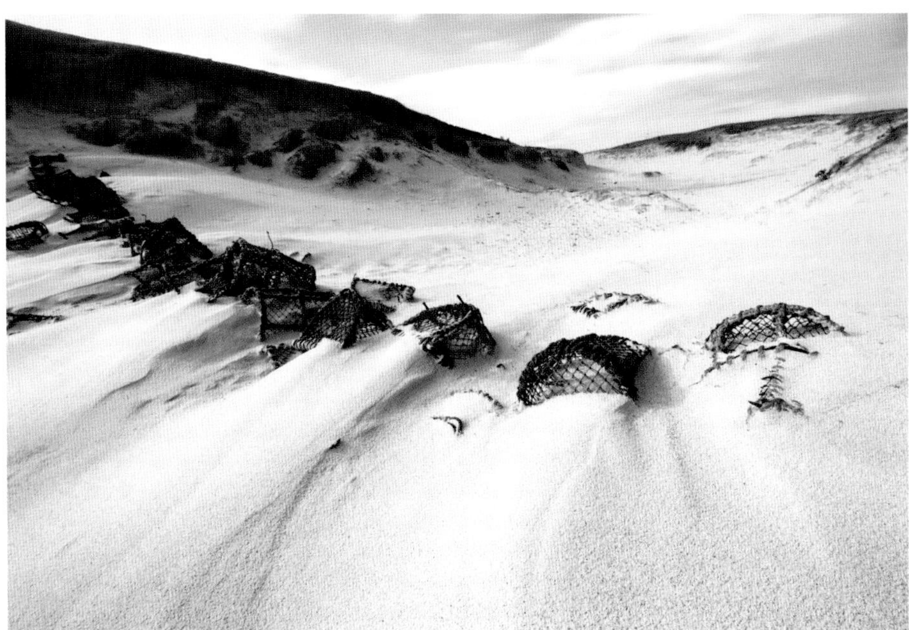

Old creels strung across dunes on Vatersay

Right: Fishing boat, Vatersay Bay

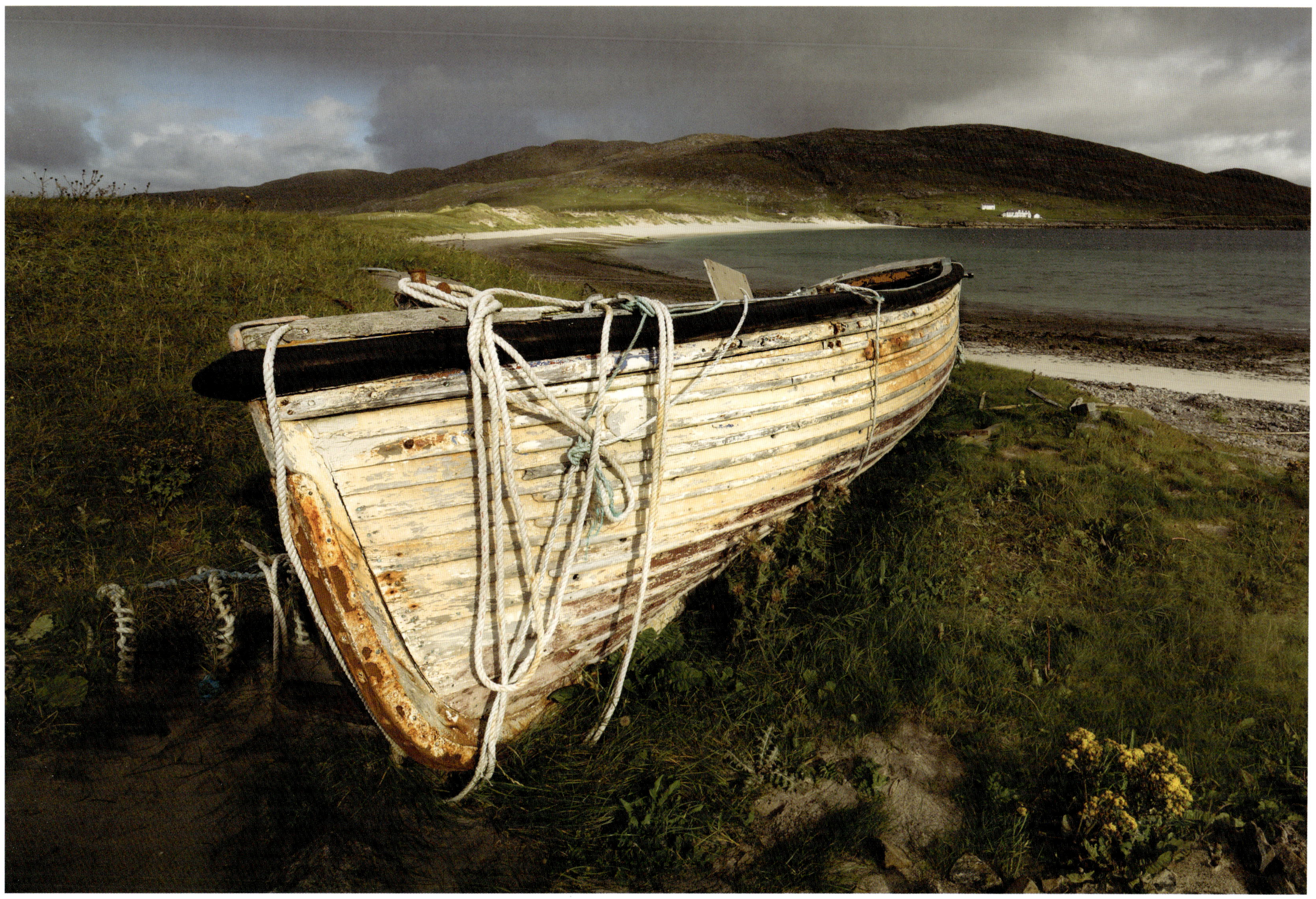

Going Nowhere

For many years, island vehicles and machinery that could no longer be coaxed into service had nowhere specific to go. They couldn't be disposed of in vast landfills or carted off to scrapyards, as on the mainland. Towed to their final resting place, they'd end up on the roadside or in gardens where they'd be harvested for parts. Slowly but inexorably the elements would further dismantle them, until only the perished tyre rubber and the fused, rusting bones of their chassis and engine blocks remained.

On the northern tip of Barra, old vehicles were dragged onto the beach to shore up the eroding dunes. Their remnants can still be seen lying askew at the high-tide mark, or poking out of the sand like props on the set of an 'end of civilisation' movie. In modern times, strict environmental regulations govern many aspects of island life. Long gone are the days of machinery being left on the beach for the elements to disassemble.

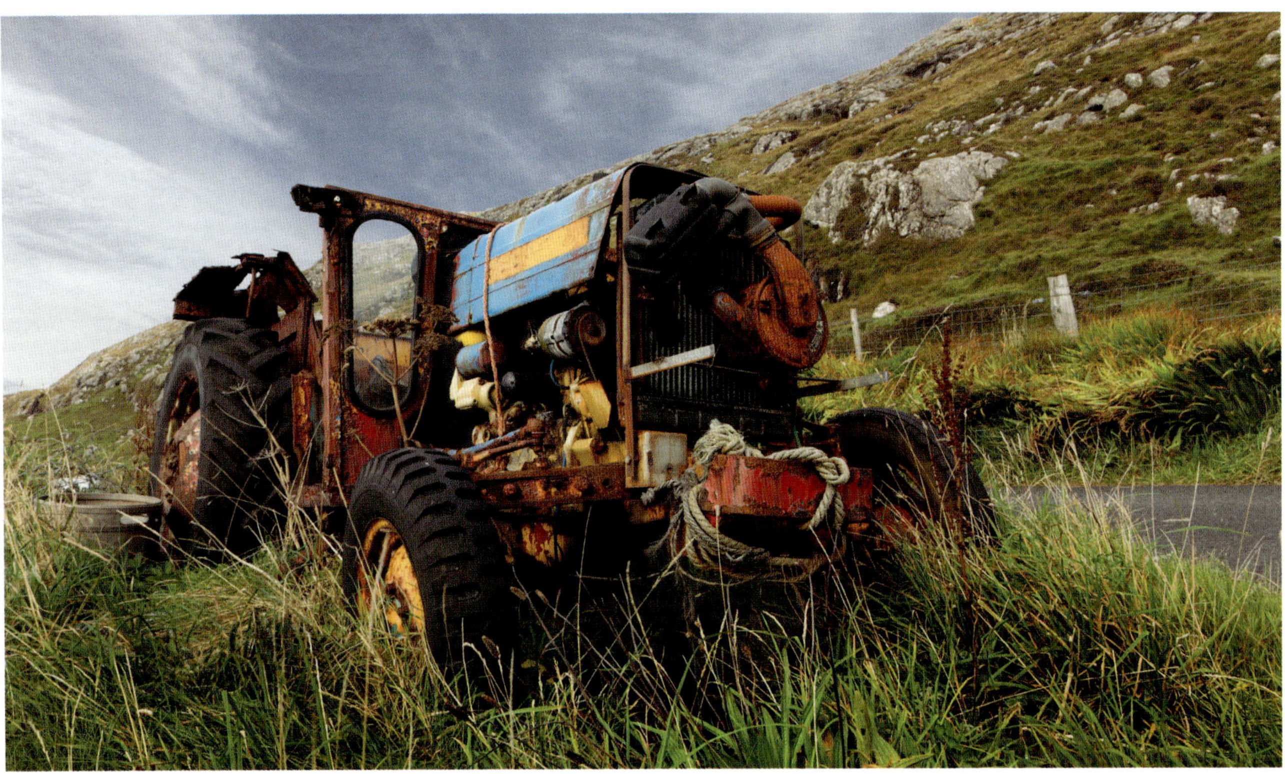

Scrapped tractor, Barra

Right: Tràigh Sgùrabhal, Barra

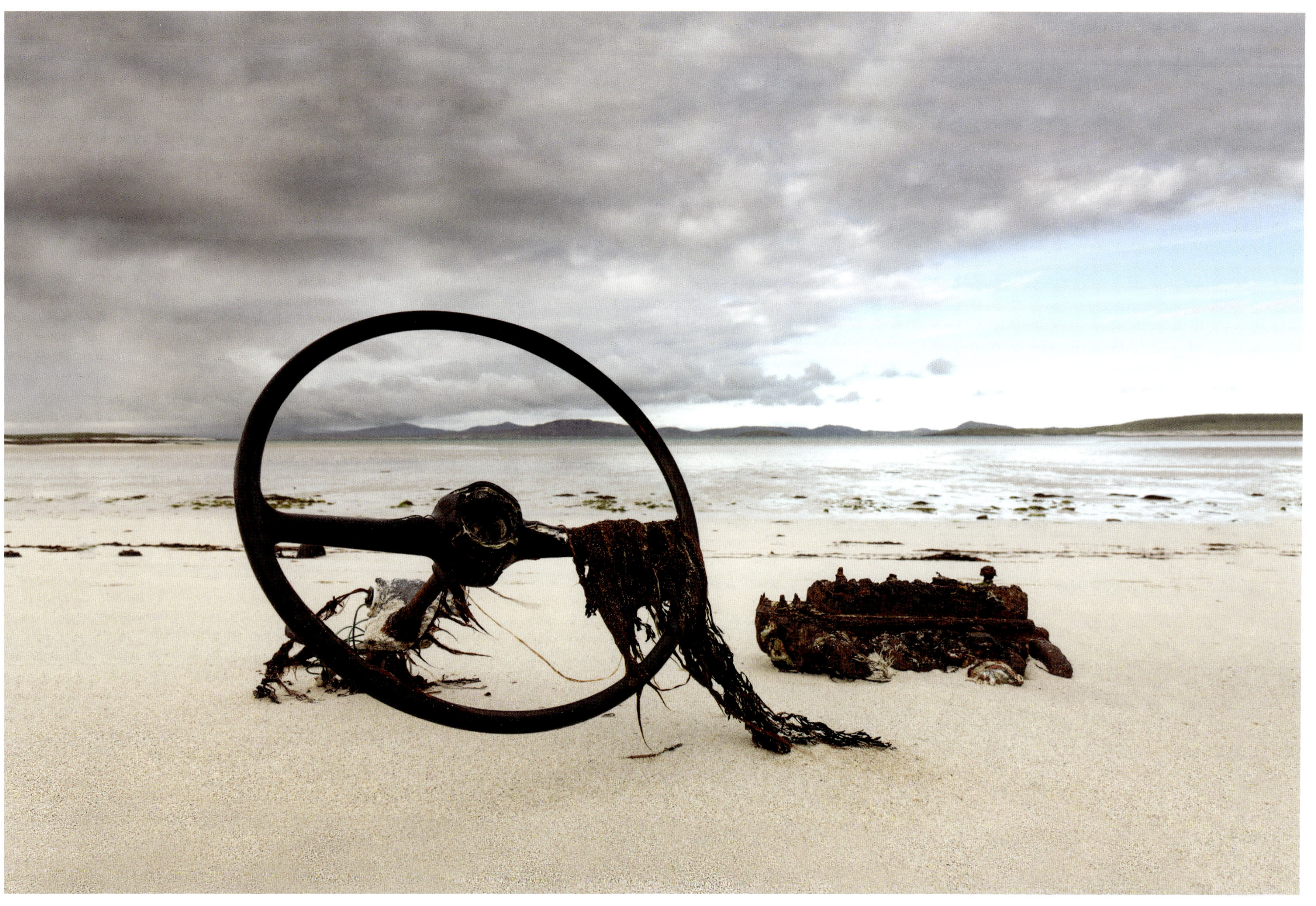

The Power of Peat

Traditionally, much of the islands' distinctly flavoured fresh water came filtered through the tannin-rich blanket bogs of peat. The many rectangular depressions in the bogs mark the peat cuttings that were once the chief source of fuel for cooking and heating until mains electricity finally came to the islands in 1967.

Blanket peat bog is a globally rare environment, only found in cool, wet, oceanic climates. The peat bogs of the Western Isles began to form when plant material laid down around 4,300 years ago was partially preserved in the acidic, waterlogged land. Today the bogs can be several metres deep and are mostly covered by sphagnum moss, heather, and deer grass. Stained waters run off the bogs adding to the rich palette of the landscape, colouring the rocks and seams of white crystal a warm russet. At Tràigh Tuath on Barra's west coast, the tea-coloured waters run down from the valley and snake across the white sand into the blue Atlantic.

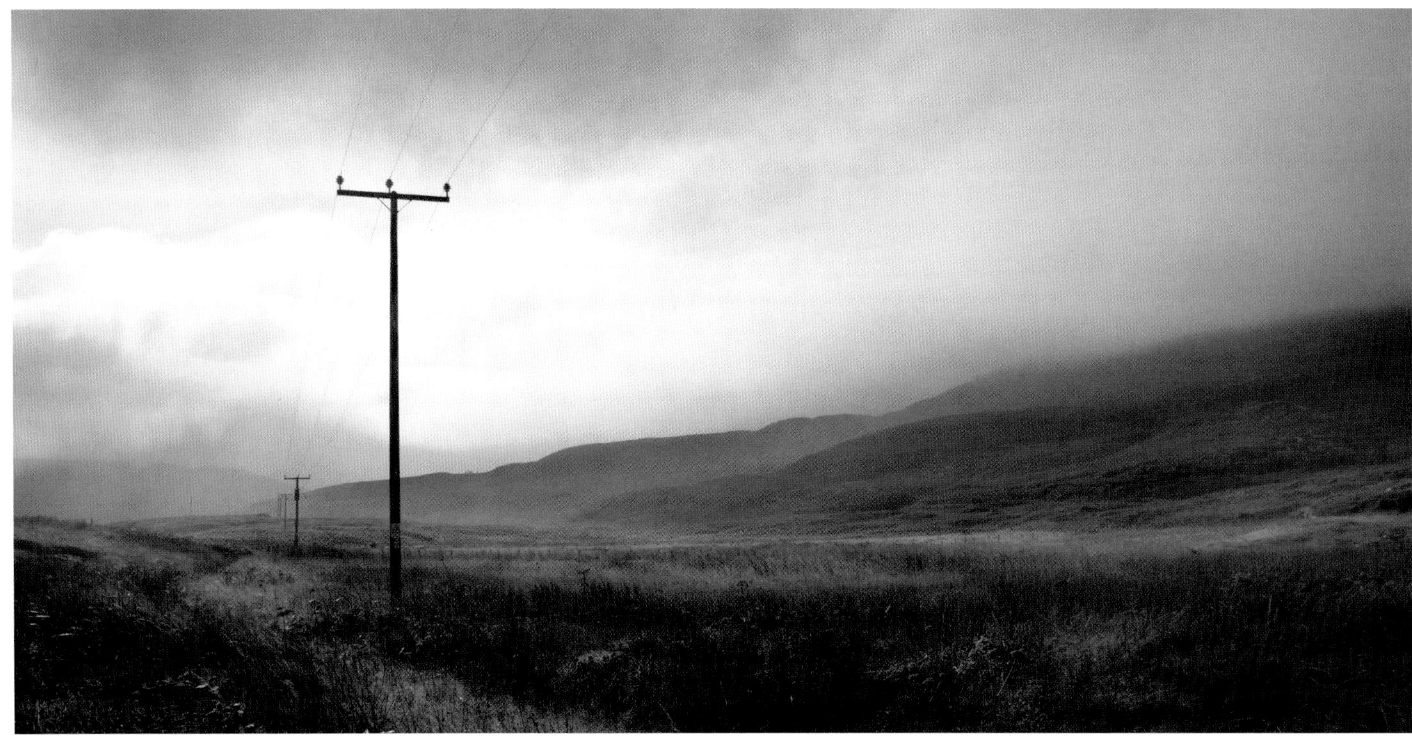

Electricity lines run over the blanket bog, which used to provide the main source of fuel on the islands

Right: Tannin-stained river, Tràigh Tuath, Barra

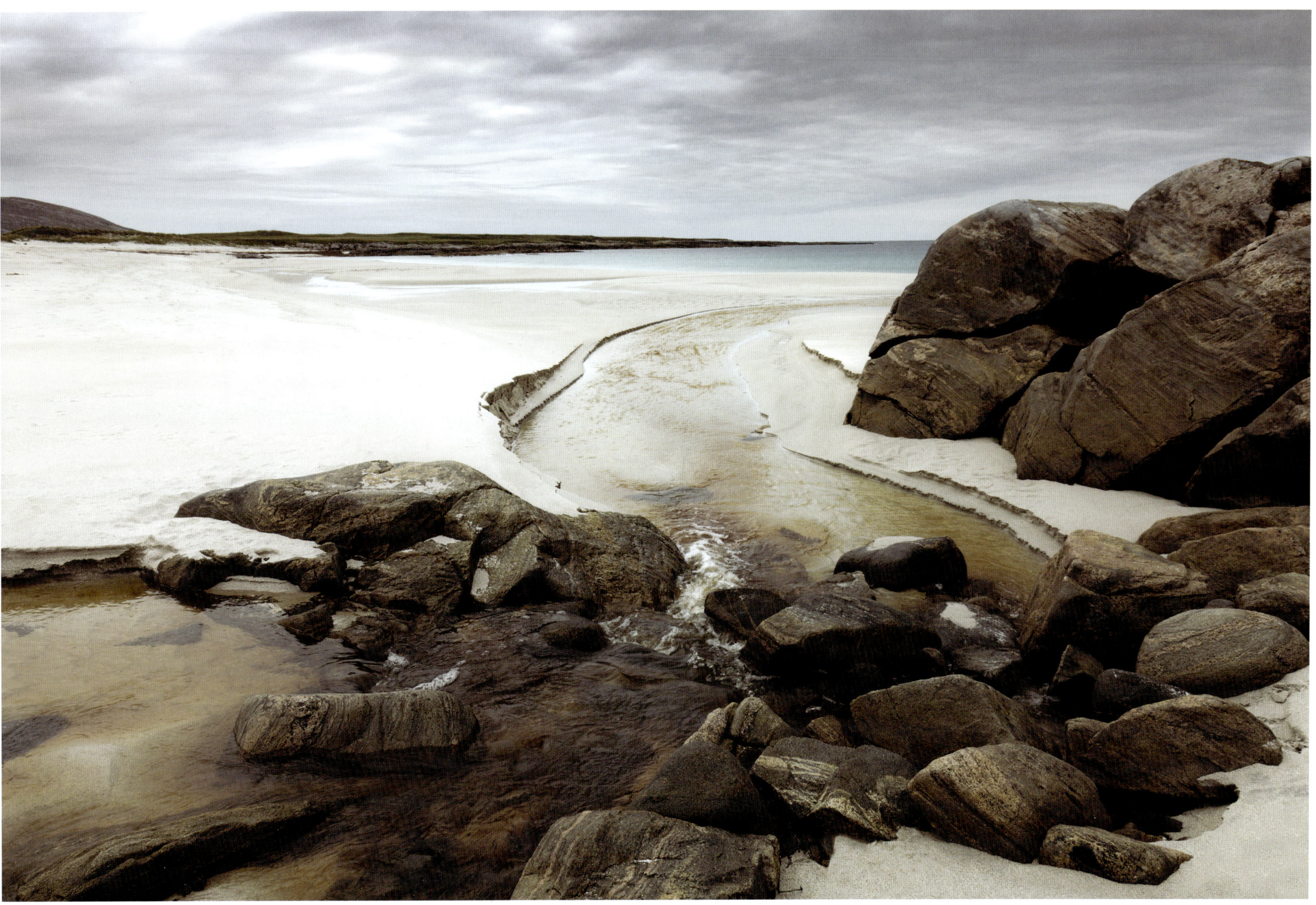

Home No More

The many abandoned crofters' cottages are part of the character of the isles. They are like museum exhibits with the added appeal of being in situ, and exploring them can be highly evocative. With a little imagination, standing by an old hearth and surveying the view through glassless windows, you can get a fleeting sense of what life may have been like for the families who used to call the cottages home.

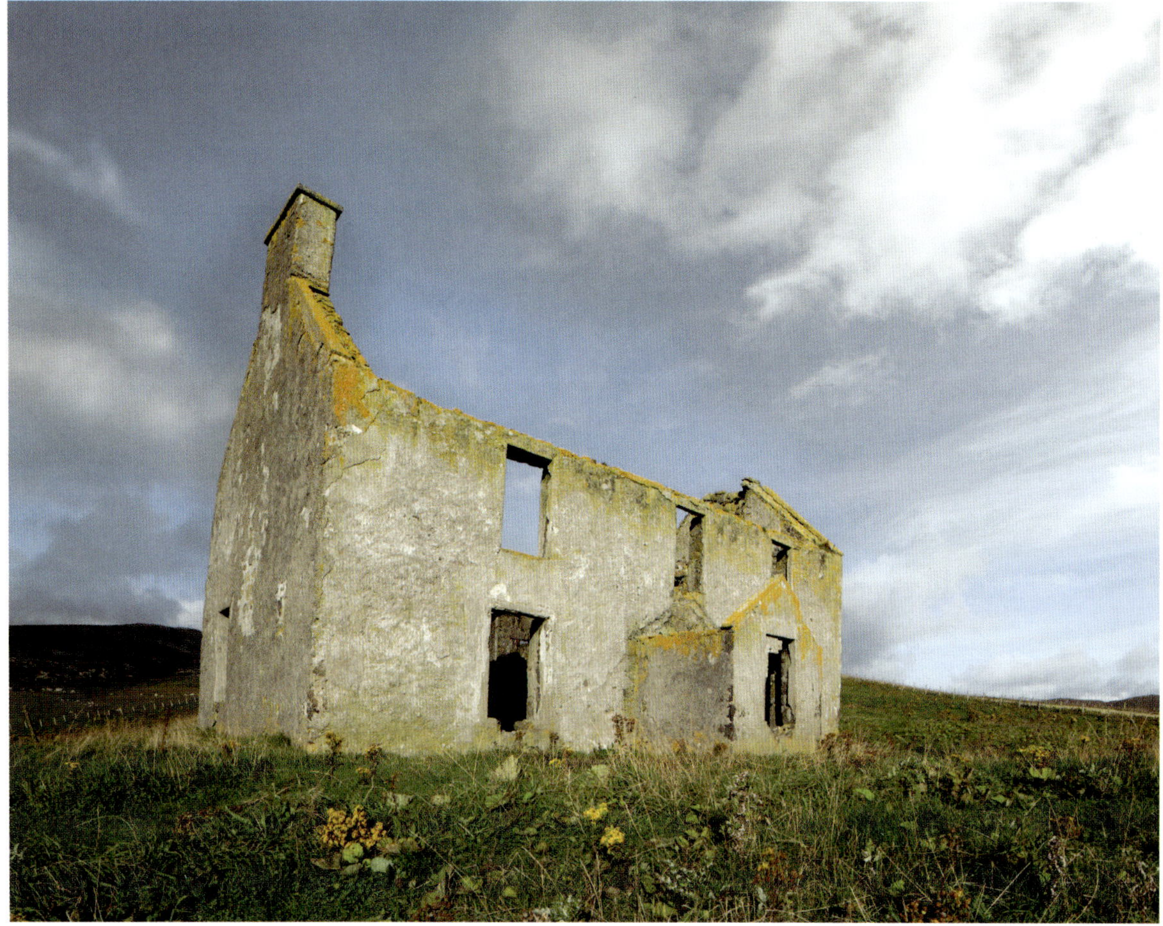

The shell of Vatersay House

The ruins of the once substantial Vatersay House overlook the main settlement on the island. Formerly the home of the tenant farmer, known as the tacksman, the house was built during the period in which the land was owned by notorious highland clearer Colonel John Gordon of Cluny. In 1853, it was used to shelter some of the survivors of the *Annie Jane* shipwreck.

At the south-eastern tip of the island is the deserted village of Eòrasdail. Established by fishermen from the abandoned isle of Mingulay to the south, it was itself abandoned in the 1970s.

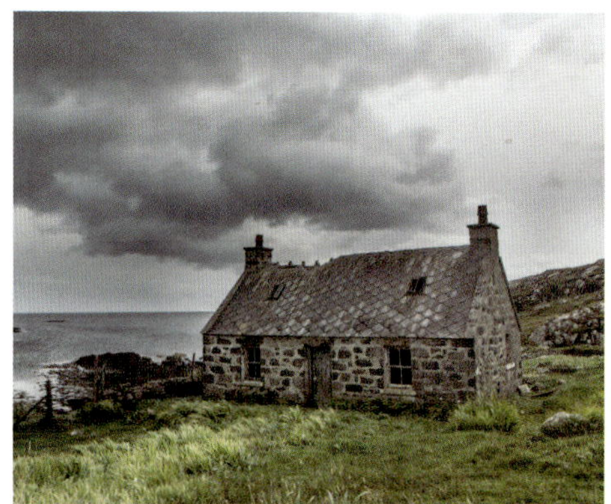

Abandoned cottage, Uidh

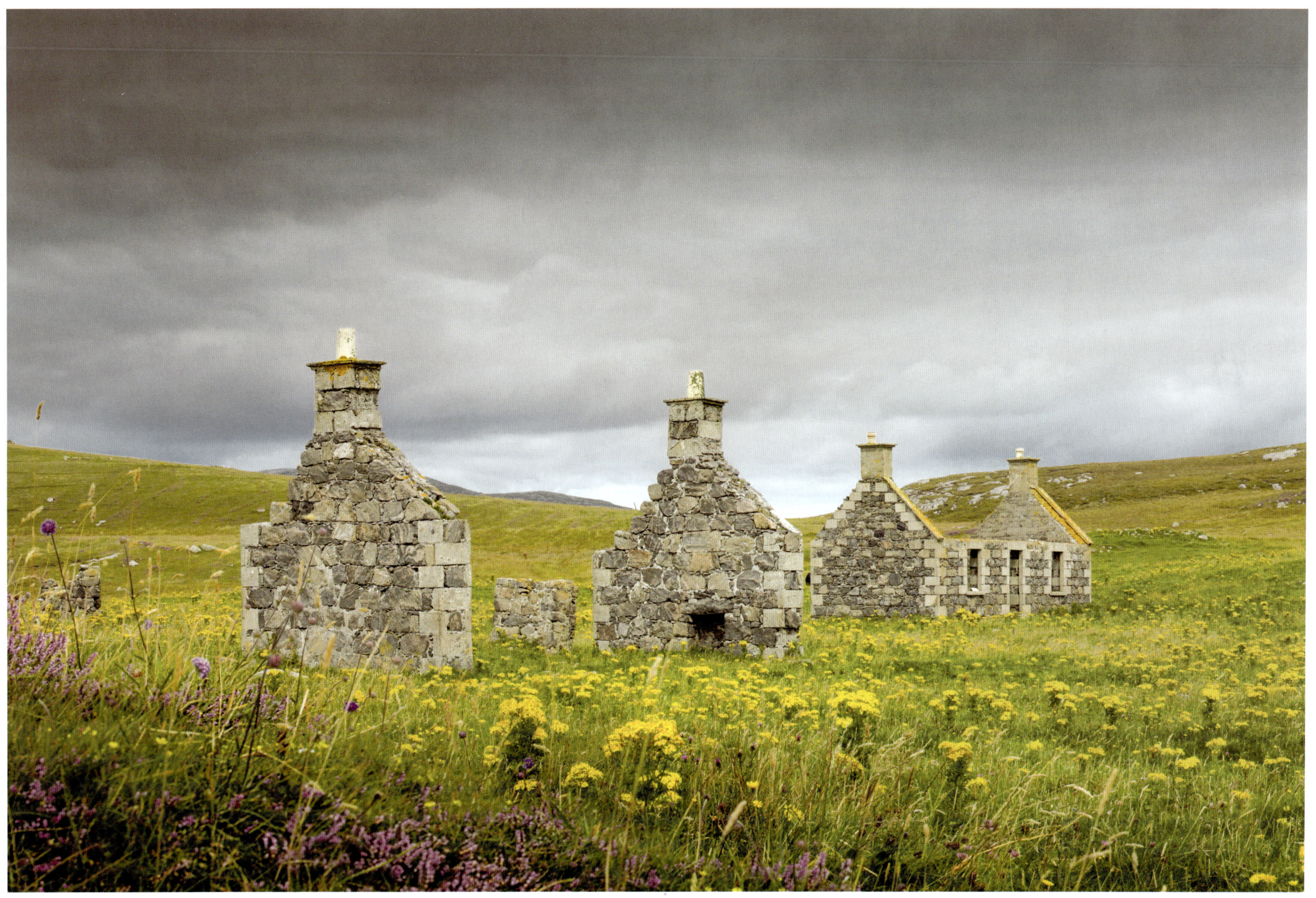

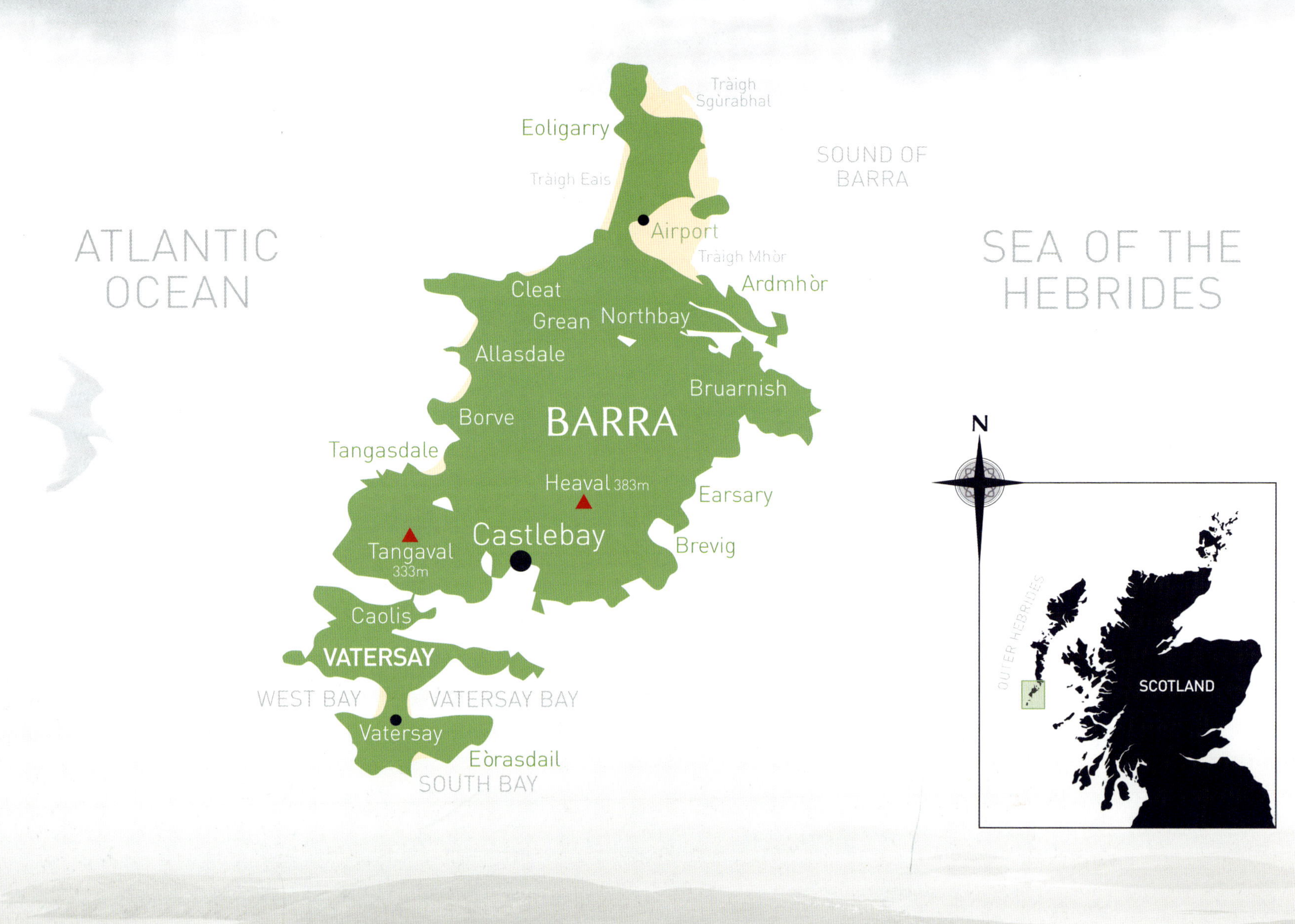

ATLANTIC
OCEAN
SEA OF THE
HEBRIDES
Tràigh Sgùrabhal
Eoligarry
Tràigh Eais
SOUND OF
BARRA
Airport
Tràigh Mhòr
Ardmhòr
Cleat
Grean
Northbay
Allasdale
Bruarnish
Borve
BARRA
Tangasdale
Heaval 383m
Earsary
Tangaval
333m
Castlebay
Brevig
Caolis
VATERSAY
WEST BAY
VATERSAY BAY
Vatersay
Eòrasdail
SOUTH BAY
N
OUTER HEBRIDES
SCOTLAND